Bernard Meyer's East Coast Cuisine

Bernard Meyer

An Atlantic Insight Book

Formac Publishing Company Limited

1988

Canadian Cataloguing in Publication Data
Meyer, Bernard, 1950-
  Bernard Meyer's East Coast Cuisine
  Includes index.   ISBN 0-88780-063-7
1. Cookery, French.   1. Title.
TX719.M49 1988   641.5944   C88-098553-4

Front cover photograph: Eric Hayes

An Atlantic Insight Book
East Coast Chefs 1

Formac Publishing Company Limited
5359 Inglis Street
Halifax, Nova Scotia B3H 1J4

Published with the assistance of the Nova Scotia Department of Culture, Recreation and Fitness

Printed and bound in Canada

CONTENTS

Acknowledgements

I wish to thank all those people who assisted in the preparation of this book of recipes. Without your support and encouragement, it would not have become a reality.

In particular I would like to thank my mother, Jeanne, and my grandmother, Antoinette, who introduced me to cuisine and who helped me to see the beauty of the profession.

Thanks to my friends in Nova Scotia who supported me and understood my philosophy. And I thank those I have met who were able to distinguish the difference between good cuisine and fine cuisine.

Finally, I wish to thank that special friend I discovered here in Nova Scotia and whose rich support I will never forget.

To my very best friend, in and out of the kitchen.

Introduction

This collection of recipes is a personal statement. It is an act of sharing, as well as communicating knowledge. I recorded these recipes in the hope that you, too, may experience a sharing, and enjoy moments of wonder and delight.

This cookbook is me, my cuisine, my stamp. It is something I've always wanted to do. It is the giving away of a continuity. As a child, at home, we had a farm where the spirit of the garden was always there. The attention to planting and tending, wondering if spring would bring enough food for the fall, whether or not the vegetables and herbs would ripen in time for harvest.

Home is the Alsace region of France where the villages are peopled by wine growers who take great pride in the quality and individuality of their product. This background has been the inspiration for my cuisine. The feelings are the same, the material is as rich and as strong. Here I learned how to appreciate the raw materials and the details.

It began early for me. At the age of nine, while attending boarding school in Paris, I was solely responsible for a dining room which served sixty students. Looking at all the activity going on in the kitchen, it was already a sensation, an anticipation as I observed the timing of all the movements. By the time I was 16, I turned to cuisine as a profession, and eventually found work with some of the established masters.

By the late 1970s, I felt I had learned all the proper basics. Yet, there were other goals, particularly the evasive ones of self-fulfillment and recognition as a master in my own right. I set out to do this in Nova Scotia in 1981.

At first, the adjustment to a new country and an unfamiliar language was difficult. But the language of cuisine transcends any practical barriers. For me, those years were the hardest. It was a new education, a new apprenticeship, and I realize today that it was not just me, but the people here, who helped me to achieve success.

After settling in, I found a new outlook on the artistic possibilities of cuisine. My original preparations mirrored not only my personal style, but also reflected Nova Scotia and Canada. My approach to quality cuisine, using local produce, required the development of a knowledgeable support system. Soon it became a philosophy.

There are two types of cuisine, a good one and a bad one. The subtle differences can be learned and felt. You can't invent food or eating, but you can take that basic function and elevate it to an art. You create with existing chemistry. Cuisine becomes a matter of discovery, a chemistry of understanding.

But I also want to be approachable, both with this cookbook and in my daily routines. This exists, especially in the countryside near Digby where I am *chef de cuisine* at The Pines. Around a kitchen table, there is always something being shared. Whether it is food or drink or conversation, it is here we share the sorrows and pleasures of our existence. Life is wine and food and friends. In trying these recipes, you are partaking in a rich tradition of cuisine.

Bernard Francis Meyer, Cuisinier
The Pines, Digby, N.S.

SOUPS

Cold *Madrilène Royale*

A dish which is absolutely dazzling during the summer months.

1 cup whipped cream - 250 ml
1 onion, diced
28 oz. stewed tomatoes - 795 ml
2 tsp. tomato paste - 10 ml
2 cups chicken stock - 500 ml
1/2 cup *roux* - 125 ml
1 cup tomato *concassé* - 250 ml
salt and pepper
Worcestershire sauce
Roux
1/2 cup butter - 125 g
1/2 cup flour - 125 g

Prepare the chicken stock according to the recipe for Clarified Chicken Consommé in this chapter. Sauté the onions in butter and add the stewed tomatoes, tomato paste and chicken stock. Bring the mixture to a boil.

Make the *roux* by kneading the flour and butter together into little balls with your fingers, enough to equal about 1/2 cup. They should have a fairly dry consistency. Away from the heat, whisk the *roux* into the tomato mixture, then let it cook for 10 minutes.

Strain the soup. Let it cool and season with salt, pepper and Worcestershire sauce. Fold in the whipped cream and serve on ice garnished with tomato *concassé* (roughly chopped tomato) and a sprig of parsley. Serves 6.

Cold Shrimp Soup

On an agreeable summer evening, this dish can provide a delightful accent of *fraîcheur*.

2 cups cooked shrimp - 500 ml
1 seedless cucumber, peeled
1 tsp. green onion - 5 ml
1 tsp. Dijon mustard - 5 ml
2 cups buttermilk - 500 ml
pinch of nutmeg

Put all the ingredients in a blender and blend until smooth. Serve on ice. Garnish with a lemon wedge, one or two whole shrimp and a sprinkle of chopped parsley. Serves 5.

Cold Wine Soup

3 cups apple juice - 750 ml
2 cups white wine - 500 ml
4 tsp. sugar - 20 ml
1 tsp. cornstarch - 5 ml
1 cinnamon stick
rind and juice of 1 lemon

Bring the apple juice to a boil. Add the cinnamon stick. Thicken with the cornstarch and sugar and let cool. Add the wine, lemon juice and rind. Serve on ice and garnish with a sprig of parsley and lemon rind. Serves 4.

Cold Strawberry Soup

An amazing dish. From time to time I add to it a purée of peaches.

4 cups fresh strawberries - 1 L
1 cup sugar syrup - 250 ml
(1 1/2 cups water and 9 tbsp. sugar)
juice from one fresh lemon
2 cloves
1 bay leaf
1/3 cup sugar - 80 ml
pinch of mace
pinch of marjoram
cornstarch

Make a sugar syrup by simmering the 1 1/2 cups of water and 9 tbsp. of sugar in a saucepan until the sugar dissolves. Bring it to a boil. Boil for 1 minute. Let the mixture cool, then strain it. Add 1 cup of the syrup to the other ingredients, except the cornstarch, and simmer for 15 minutes. Thicken to the desired consistency with cornstarch. Remove from the heat and process in a blender until smooth. Add the 1/3 cup of sugar and cook again for 5 minutes until the sugar is dissolved. Cool and serve on ice. Garnish with fresh strawberries. Serves 4.

Variations: substitute strawberries with other fruit using the same method as for strawberry soup.

Cold Watercress Soup

A marvelous touch to a summer meal. With a generous amount of cream, this soup is a delight.

3 whole leeks, sliced
1 medium-sized onion, chopped
2 tsp. butter - 10 ml
3 potatoes, sliced
3 cups *fond blanc* (white stock)- 750 ml
2 cups cream - 500 ml
1 bunch watercress, cooked and puréed
1 cup grated apple - 250 ml
1 whole lemon
salt
Worcestershire sauce

Sauté the leeks, onions and potatoes very lightly in the butter. Add the *fond blanc* (see the recipe for White Chicken Stock in this chapter). Let it simmer for half an hour or until the potatoes are cooked. Pass the mixture through a strainer and let it cool. Stir in the cream. Add salt, juice from 1 lemon, Worcestershire sauce and watercress which has been cooked in water and then put through a blender. Blend in the grated apple. Serve on ice. Garnish with fresh watercress leaves. Serves 4.

Fruit Soup I

1 medium-sized ripe banana
3-15-oz. frozen strawberries
(thawed and well drained)
 or 1 1/2 cups fresh strawberries - 227 g
1 fresh peach
1/2 apple
2 slices of fresh pineapple
4 apricot halves
1 1/2 tbsp. icing sugar - 22 ml
strained juice of 1 orange
strained juice of 1/2 lemon
apricot juice
2 tbsp. unsalted butter, melted - 20 ml
1/2 cup whipping cream - 125 ml

Wash, peel and cut all the fruit (except the frozen strawberries). Place the fruit in a blender or food processor with the icing sugar, orange juice, lemon juice, some apricot juice and the melted butter. Process for a couple of minutes. Strain and serve in chilled bowls. If holding the soup for a period of time, place the bowls on a bed of ice. Garnish with whipped cream and slices of fresh fruit. Serves 4.

Fruit Soup II

1 1/2 cups water - 375 ml
9 tbsp. granulated sugar - 135 ml
zest of 1 deep-coloured orange, finely grated

5 medium-sized ripe bananas
juice of 1 1/2 lemons
2 tbsp. unsalted butter - 30 ml
1 1/2 tbsp. icing sugar - 22 ml
1 1/2 cups whipping cream - 375 ml
3-15 oz. frozen strawberries, well drained - 3-426 g
1 1/2 cups pineapple yogurt - 375 ml
juice of 3 oranges

Combine the water and sugar in a saucepan. Place on medium heat and stir until the sugar is dissolved. Bring it to a boil and boil for 1 minute. Add the orange zest. Let the mixture cool. Strain the syrup.

Purée 3 of the bananas. Add the lemon juice and melted butter plus the icing sugar. Hold at room temperature to prevent the butter from solidifying. Whip the cream in a chilled bowl and fold it into the banana purée. Do not overmix. Hold the cream-banana mixture in the fridge. It will be formed into small dumplings at serving time.

Purée the remaining 2 bananas. Add the strawberries, yogurt and orange juice purée. Add the cooled syrup purée again for a few seconds. Pour into chilled soup bowls. Garnish with fresh strawberries, sliced kiwi, fresh pineapple, melon balls or any combination of these or other appropriate fruit. Top with the whipped cream-banana dumplings made by rolling the cream mixture between two spoons. Serve *very* cold. Serves 8 to 10.

Jellied Consommé

2 cups consommé - 500 ml
1 tbsp. gelatin powder - 15 ml

Add between 1 and 2 tbsp. of gelatin powder to 2 cups of consommé, (see the recipe for Clarified Consommé in this chapter). Bring to a boil. Remove from the heat and let cool overnight. Serve on ice with a sprig of parsley and a lemon wedge. Serves 4.

Jellied Grapefruit and Avocado Soup

2 avocados, peeled and the pit removed
1/4 cup whipped cream - 60 ml
1/4 cup grapefruit juice - 60 ml
3 cups jellied chicken consommé
salt
chili powder

Blend the peeled and pitted avacados in a blender. Add the cream, grapefruit juice and blend together. Season with salt and chili powder to taste. Add to the jellied chicken consommé (see the recipe for Clarified Chicken Consommé in this chapter). Serve the soup on ice. Garnish with grapefruit sections and whipped cream. Serves 4.

Mussel Soup

A dish which goes well with every season, this soup is especially nice during the winter months.

4 tbsp. chopped shallot - 60 ml
2 cups whipping cream - 475 ml
2 cups white wine - 475
1 cup chicken stock - 250 ml
1 cup fish stock - 250 ml
1 handful fresh parsley
2 bunches fresh chervil
1 small bunch fresh chives
2 lbs. mussels (small, cleaned)
salt and pepper to taste

Sauté the shallots in butter. Steam the previously washed mussels until cooked, then add the white wine. Remove the mussels from their shells.

Meanwhile reduce the mussel stock to one-third its volume. Add the chicken stock and fish stock (see the recipes in this chapter). Alternatively, use a chicken bouillon cube to make the chicken stock. Reduce the mixture again. Remove from the heat. Add the cream and cool the mixture. Once chilled, strain and add the chopped herbs. Season to taste. Place the reserved mussels in the creamy liquid. Serves 5.

Billy Bye Soup

A classic from my repertoire which I often interpret with a touch of local shellfish and fresh herbs from my garden.

2 lbs. clams - 908 g
2 tbsp. finely chopped shallot - 30 ml
1/4 cup finely chopped onion - 60 ml
a few sprigs each of parsley and dill
bay leaf
1/2 cup dry white wine - 125 ml
1/2 cup celery and carrots in julienne strips - 125 ml
1 tbsp. butter - 30 ml
2 cups fish stock - 500 ml
3/4 cup double cream
1 egg yolk mixed with a little cream
a little curry powder
salt
freshly ground pepper
4 truffle slices, cut into julienne strips
a little fresh chervil

Scrape the clams. Brush them and wash them thoroughly. Put the clams, finely chopped shallot, onion, herbs and white wine in a covered pot. Bring to a boil and allow it to simmer for 5 minutes. Take the clams out of the shells, remove the beard and strain the liquid through a cloth.

Sweat the julienne of vegetables in butter. Add the fish stock (see the recipe in this chapter) and the clam stock. Cook for 1 minute, then remove from the heat. Add the cream. Put the clams into the soup, and bind with the egg yolk and cream mixture. Season the soup with salt and freshly ground pepper. Serves 4.

Fish Chowder

The interpretations of fish chowder seem infinite. This is mine. Try with your own modifications.

3 tbsp. clear bacon fat - 45 ml
2 carrots
1 medium-sized onion
1 clove garlic
3/4 cup shredded white cabbage - 185 ml
3/4 cup leeks, white part only - 185 ml
3/4 cup spinach - 185 ml
1/2 tomato
2 medium-sized potatoes
3 cups fish stock - 750 ml
1 cup whipping cream - 250 ml
seasoning to taste
fish, mixture of halibut, scallops, salmon, etc.

Cut all the vegetables *à la paysanne*. Sauté all except the potatoes, in bacon fat. Add the hot fish stock and simmer for 20 minutes. Add the potatoes and cream and allow the mixture to reduce by simmering for an additional 10 minutes.

Cut the fish into large julienne strips or large cubes and sauté in a little of the fish stock just long enough for it to remain firm. Strain the stock from the sauté into the soup. Add the fish and adjust the seasoning. Serves 6.

Monkfish Stew with Saffron

This is a local fish which we have a tendency to forget. It is especially nice pan-fried, but it combines well with the salmon and saffron for a unique dish that stands alone as a main course.

3/4 lb. boneless monkfish - 340 g
1/3 lb. boneless salmon - 151 g
3 cloves garlic
4 fresh basil leaves
2 tbsp. little peas, shelled - 30 ml
2 tbsp. lima beans - 30 ml
1 1/2 tbsp. olive oil - 22 ml
3 pinches powdered saffron
3 tbsp. vegetable bouillon - 45 ml
1/2 cup heavy cream - 125 ml
1 pinch saffron threads
1/4 lemon
salt and pepper to taste

Cut the monkfish once lengthwise and then 5 times crosswise to make 12 pieces, each about 1 1/2 inches by 1 1/4 inches in size. Cut the salmon into 1/2-inch cubes. Mince the garlic. Cut the basil leaves into thin strips. Shell the peas and beans and cook the peas for 10 minutes in boiling salted water adding the beans at 8 minutes. Drain.

Put 1 tbsp. of the olive oil into a small saucepan over medium heat, add the garlic and 1 pinch of the powdered saffron and cook for 3 minutes. Add the vegetable bouillon, the cream and the pinch of saffron threads and continue to cook (barely boiling) for 2 minutes. Check the seasoning and squeeze in lemon juice to taste, about 1 1/2 tsp. Add the beans and little peas and keep warm over very low heat.

In a non-stick pan, heat the remaining 1/2 tbsp. olive oil over high heat. Season the monkfish and the salmon with salt, pepper and 2 pinches of powdered saffron. Sauté the monkfish for 3 minutes. Remove the monkfish to warm plates and sauté the salmon, stirring constantly, for 30 seconds.

For the presentation, arrange the salmon around the monkfish on warmed plates. Nap the fish with the saffron sauce and sprinkle each serving with some basil strips. Serves 4.

Soupe de Moules

Similar to the previous mussel soup but with a different presentation. Serving 10 guests, it could be a refreshing *entrée* for your garden party.

6 lbs. mussels
1 bottle Pouilly-Fuissé
3 shallots, chopped
3 1/2 tbsp. chopped parsley - 52 ml
7 tbsp. unsalted butter - 105 ml
2 to 3 lbs. leeks, cut into strips - 303 g
1 3/4 cups olive oil - 435 ml
2/3 lb. onions, minced - 303 g
6 1/2 lbs. fresh fish - 2.95 kg
3 lbs. tomatoes, seeded and cut into pieces - 1.36 kg
3 1/2 tbsp. chopped fresh fennel rib - 52 ml
2 cloves garlic, chopped
1/2 bay leaf
1 sprig thyme
1 1/2 cups cream - 375 ml
saffron
salt and pepper
grated cheese
croutons

Steam the mussels in 1/4 bottle of the white wine, with the shallots, parsley and butter, until the mussels open. Heat the olive oil in an 8- to 10-quart soup kettle. Add the onions and leeks and cook over low heat for 5 minutes. Pour in 4 quarts of water, the remaining wine and the liquid in which the mussels were cooked. Add the fish which has been cut into pieces, the tomatoes, herbs and seasonings. Cook for 40 minutes.

Pour the stock through a very fine strainer, rubbing all the ingredients to extract the juice and the flesh of the fish. Pour the stock into a smaller soup pot and bring to the boiling point. At the last moment, add the mussels and the cream. Cook for 2 minutes

Serve in a soup tureen with a side bowl of croutons made of toasted bread and grated cheese. Serves 10.

Petite Marmite

Literally translated as "little cooking pot," this is the name given to a method of serving consommé that originated in Paris about a hundred years ago. The soup was served in the earthenware pot in which it was cooked, along with rusks or bread slices dried in the oven then spread with marrow.

3/4 lb. top of rump - 340 g
1/2 lb. rib of beef - 227 g
1/4 lb. marrow bone - 125 g
2 sets chicken giblets
2 to 3 small carrots
1 small turnip
2 to 3 leeks, white part only cut into chunks
2 small onions
1/4 head of celery
1/4 small head of cabbage
10 cups simple consommé, cold - 2 1/2 L

Put the meat, the marrow bone (wrapped in a piece of muslin) and the cold consommé (see the recipe this chapter) into a pan. Bring to the boil and skim.

Add the carrots and turnip cut into a uniform size and shape (blanch the vegetables if they are old). The leeks should be cut in chunks and blanched; small onions must be lightly cooked on the stove; the celery, blanched and cut into small pieces.

Blanch the cabbage and roll it into a tight ball. Instead of being cooked in the pot, the cabbage can be blanched separately in stock and added to the consommé just before serving.

Simmer the meat and vegetables together very gently for 4 hours, adding a little stock from time to time to make up for the loss of liquid by evaporation. An hour before serving, add the chicken giblets and continue cooking. The chicken giblets can be browned in the oven before being put into the stock .

Remove the surplus fat, but bear in mind that *petite marmite* should have a few light circlets of fat on the surface. Remove the marrow bone, unwrap the muslin and put the bone back into the pot.

Serve the *petite marmite* with bread, sliced and dried in the oven, or with rusks. Serves 6.

Seafood Chowder

2 oz. codfish - 50 g
2 oz. haddock - 50 g
2 oz. salmon - 50 g
2 oz. halibut - 50 g
2 oz. scallops - 50 g
1/2 cup unsalted butter - 125 ml
8 cups fish stock - 2 L
6 oz. white wine
salt and pepper
2 large potatoes
2 large carrots
1/2 leek
1 large Spanish onion
1 1/2 tbsp. bacon fat - 22 ml
1 tbsp. oil - 15 ml
1/2 cup flour - 125 ml
1 cup whipping cream - 250 ml
fresh herbs

Cut all the vegetables into medium-sized cubes and sauté them in half of the butter, oil and bacon fat. Once cooked, pour the fish stock (see the recipe in this chapter) over the vegetables and bring to a boil.

Gently heat the remaining fat and add flour to thicken. Strain the fish stock over this mixture and bring to a boil until a spoon-coating consistency is reached.

Pour the liquid over the vegetables. Add the chopped herbs, white wine and cream. Mix together. If the consistency is too heavy, add more stock. Serve very hot. Serves 10.

Consommé
Strong Clarified Stock

Consommé is a beef or chicken concoction that, when perfectly made, is a beautifully clear and sparkling soup. It can be enjoyed as is, or used as a base for other soups, for sauces or for aspic. It has all the protein of meat and none of the fat. There are two steps in making consommé. The first is to prepare the stock and the second is to clarify it. Clarification is the simple process that gives consommé its crystal-clear appearance.

A very strong consommé, or *consommé double*, is made by adding meat to the clarification and cooking it for 1 hour, thus concentrating the flavour in the liquid. A cold *consommé double* should be gelatinous without being too firm. With the addition of tomato, it becomes the celebrated *Consommé à la Madrilène*.

1 unpeeled onion, halved
4 lbs. beef bones - 1.82 kg
(or a mixture of beef and chicken bones)
1 bay leaf
1 tsp. black peppercorns - 5 ml
1 medium-sized onion
(peeled and stuck with 3 cloves)
2 tsp. salt - 10 ml

Place the split onion, cut sides down, in an iron skillet over medium heat. Let it cook until the onion burns and is very black. It is essential that the onion is burnt on the cut sides. It will cook with the bones for hours to produce the amber colour a consommé should have.

Place all the other ingredients in a large kettle and cover them with cold water. Bring to a boil, skimming any scum that forms on the surface. After it boils, lower the heat and simmer slowly for 6 hours. Strain.

During the cooking, add water if there is too much evaporation. There should be 12 cups of liquid remaining. Let it cool and remove the fat from the surface.

The consommé

1 cup cold water - 250 ml
1 lb. very lean ground beef - 454 ml
6 egg whites
1/2 cup diced celery leaves - 125 ml
3/4 cup diced tomato - 185 ml
2 cups sliced green of leek, - 500 ml
or 1 cup green of scallions
1/2 cup coarsely cut parsley and tarragon - 125 ml
3/4 cup sliced carrots - 185 ml
1/2 tsp. black peppercorns - 2 ml
2 bay leaves
1/2 tsp. thyme leaves - 2 ml
salt, if necessary
12 cups of stock - 3 L

In a large kettle, combine all the ingredients except the stock. Add the stock and bring to a boil over high heat, stirring constantly to avoid sticking. Don't worry if the stock becomes very cloudy and a white foam forms. The albumin in the egg whites and meat is solidifying, and this is the process that will clarify the stock. When the mixture comes to a boil, *stop stirring* and reduce the heat to a simmer. As the mixture simmers, you will notice that the ingredients form a "crust" on the surface of the liquid with one or two holes, through which the liquid erupts, boiling slightly.

Allow the consommé to simmer gently for 1 hour without disturbing the little "geysers" in any way. Turn off the heat and let the consommé settle for 15 minutes.

Strain the consommé through a sieve lined with a paper napkin, taking care not to disturb the crust. Tilt the pan to one side so that all the liquid pours out.

After the consommé has rested for an hour, check to see if there is any fat on the surface. If so, remove it by blotting the top with paper towels. The consommé can be served hot or cold.

With different garnishes, consommé takes on different names, such as *celestine* with the addition of shredded crêpes, or *royale* with cubes of meat-flavoured custard. The crust is usually discarded, but by adding beaten eggs, bread crumbs and seasonings, it can be turned into a satisfying meat loaf. Be careful to remove the peppercorns for this use.

We often have a tendency to forget this classic, but a good consommé is absolutely delicious and well worth the effort.

Fond Blanc de Volaille
White Chicken Stock

**2 lb. 3 oz. chicken carcasses, necks, wings, - 1 kg
or 1 boiling fowl
1 veal knuckle bone or calf's tongue
1 cup sliced carrots - 250 ml
1 leek, white part only
8 cups water - 2 L
1/2 stalk celery
1 cup mushrooms - 250 ml
1 onion
1 clove
1 bouquet garni
2 tbsp. butter - 30 ml**

You can make chicken stock without the veal knuckle or calf's tongue, but the addition of one of these will make the stock richer and more full-bodied. It can be rather watery if you use only chicken. After the tongue has improved the stock, you can serve it as a dish in its own right, in a vinaigrette sauce or with a fresh, herb-flavoured tomato *coulis*.

Wash and finely slice the carrots, leek, celery and mushrooms. Heat the butter in a saucepan and sweat the vegetables. Add the boiling fowl or carcasses, together with the veal bone or tongue. Cover with cold water and bring to a boil. Lower the heat and simmer gently, skimming the surface frequently. After cooking for 10 minutes, add the bouquet garni and the onion spiked with the clove.

Cook for a further 2 hours and 20 minutes, then strain the stock into a bowl through a muslin-lined sieve. Set aside in a cool place. As with all stocks, do not refrigerate until it is completely cold. The stock will keep in the refrigerator for 1 week, or for several weeks in the freezer. Yields 8 cups.

Fish Stock

2 lb. 3 oz. fish bones and heads - 1 kg
(sole, turbot, whiting, conger, eel, or any white-fleshed fish)
1 medium onion
white part of 1 leek
1/2 cup mushrooms - 125 ml
1/2 cup butter - 125 ml
1/2 cup dry white wine - 125 ml
1 bouquet garni
8 cups water - 2 L

Remove the gills from the fish heads. Soak the bones and heads in cold water for 3 to 4 hours. Roughly chop the fish bones and heads. Wash and chop the vegetables and sweat them in the butter. Then add the chopped bones and heads and simmer for a few minutes. Pour in the white wine. Increase the heat and reduce the liquid by half, then cover the contents of the pan with water. Bring the mixture to the boil, skimming the surface frequently.

After 5 minutes cooking time, add the bouquet garni and simmer, uncovered, for 25 minutes. Carefully strain the stock into a bowl through a muslin-lined sieve. Leave to cool, then store in the refrigerator. The stock will keep for 1 week in the refrigerator and for several weeks in the freezer.

Consommé Rich, or Clarified Consommé

1 1/2 lbs. chopped lean beef, - 750 ml
1 large carrot, diced
1 cup diced leeks, white part only - 250 ml
1 raw egg white
12 cups vegetable stock - 3 L

Put the chopped meat, diced vegetables and egg white into a saucepan. Mix and add cold or warm stock. Bring to a boil, stirring constantly with a wooden spoon or with a whisk. When boiling is established, draw the saucepan to the edge of the burner and simmer very slowly for 1 1/2 hours. Remove the surplus fat and strain the consommé. Yields 8 cups.

Simple Chicken Consommé
Proceed as described using a small chicken, previously browned in the oven, or an equivalent quantity of chicken giblets and carcasses.

Clarified Chicken Consommé
Proceed, as described in the recipe for Clarified Consommé, using the same ingredients and adding 3 sets of chopped chicken giblets along with the beef. I also recommend adding a small chicken, previously browned in the oven, and the bones of a roast chicken, if available. The addition of chicken is almost essential to give the consommé the desired flavour. The cooked chicken can later be made up into various dishes. Yields 8 cups.

SALADS

Chicken Salad
with Curry

This mild curry salad will make a refreshing summer dish.

2 chicken breasts, cooked and diced
1/3 cup mayonnaise - 80 ml
3 tbsp. curry powder - 45 ml
1 apple diced (reserve 2 tbsp. for garnish)
1 cup whipped cream - 250 ml
lettuce for garnish
herbs for garnish, freshly chopped

Blanch the chicken breasts in hot water, then cook slowly until the chicken is done, but remains firm. Dice the meat.

Add the curry and apples to the mayonnaise (see the recipe in the chapter on Sauces). Fold in the whipped cream. Shred the lettuce. Place the salad on top and garnish with apples and herbs. Serves 4.

Warm Oyster Salad

oysters, 3 per person
2 Belgian endive
2 tomatoes, poached and peeled
1 handful watercress
1/4 lb. leeks, blanched - 125 g
7 tbsp. butter - 100 ml
1/2 cup vegetable stock - 125 ml
1 tbsp. shallots, chopped - 30 ml
6 oz. white wine - 60 ml
1/2 cup cream - 125 ml
salt and pepper to taste

Open the oysters, detach from their bottom shells and set aside with the juice.

Prepare the salad with the endive, tomatoes and watercress.

Add the butter and the blanched leeks cut into julienne strips to the vegetable stock. Simmer for a few minutes.

Poach the oysters, with the chopped shallots, in the white wine and oyster juice for a few minutes. Remove the oysters. Add the cream and reduce the liquid until it coats the back of a spoon.

Place the julienne of leeks in centre of the salad on a platter. Arrange the poached oysters on the salad. Season the warm sauce to taste and pour over salad. Serves 4.

Lobster Salad

The superb quality of this salad is similar to a dish served at *Moulin de Mougins,* Roger Vergé's three-star restaurant near Cannes, France.

2 1-lb. lobsters - 2-454 g
2 small tomatoes
1 1/2 cups snow peas, stemmed - 375 ml
1 1/2 cups green beans, stemmed - 375 ml
4 artichoke hearts
Boston lettuce
spinach

Salad
Boil the lobsters in the usual manner, for no longer than 10 minutes. Blanch, peel and seed the tomatoes and slice them very thinly. Add the snow peas and green beans to boiling water. Boil uncovered for 5 minutes. Drain and run them under cold water to retain their colour. Shell the lobsters and set aside the tail meat and the body shell. Wash and dry the spinach and lettuce.

Dressing
2 tbsp. red wine vinegar - 30 ml
2 tbsp. vegetable oil - 30 ml
1/4 tsp. Dijon mustard - 1 ml
4 tbsp. whipping cream - 60 ml
salt and pepper to taste

Place the red wine vinegar, vegetable oil, Dijon mustard, salt and pepper in a blender and blend at high speed for 1 minute. Add the cream and blend for a few more seconds. Remove to a saucepan.

Warm the dressing. Arrange the vegetables attractively on two plates, reserving space for the lobster. Slice the tail meat into *médaillons* (round slices) and place them on the plate with the vegetables. Nap the salad with the warm dressing. Garnish with half a lobster body shell. Serves 2.

Warm Fruit Salad

1 fresh peach
1/2 fresh pear
1 banana
1/2 apple
1 kiwi fruit, peeled and thickly sliced
10 fresh strawberries
2 oranges, peeled and sectioned
1/2 cup white sugar - 125 ml
2 tbsp. unsalted butter - 30 ml
juice of 1/2 lemon
2 tbsp. Grand Marnier, or orange liqueur - 30 ml
2 tbsp. Kirsch - 30 ml
4 tbsp. red currant jelly - 60 ml
juices reserved from the fresh fruits
2 scoops vanilla ice cream

Place a frying pan over medium heat. Melt the sugar and butter and caramelize until golden brown. Add the peach, pear, banana, apple and orange sections. Sauté gently and quickly until the fruit is barely soft. Add the strawberries and kiwi and continue to sauté just long enough to coat the fruit. Do not overcook to the point where the fruits lose their vivid colours.

Arrange the prepared fruit, varying the colours, to completely circle the plate, leaving a space in the center for ice cream.

Add the lemon juice, Grand Marnier, Kirsch, the juices of the fruits and the red currant jelly to the frying pan. Caramelize over slow heat for 2 to 3 minutes. Add the ice cream to the plate, pour the sauce over the salad and ice cream and serve immediately. Serves 2.

SAUCES

Beurre Blanc and Variations

White Foamy Butter Sauce

I work a lot with *beurre blanc* and vary the recipe by adding stocks or different purées or herbs.

1 cup dry white wine - 250 ml
4 to 5 large shallots, peeled and finely diced
1/2 tsp. white pepper - 2 ml
1/2 cup white wine vinegar - 125 ml
1/3 cup whipping cream - 80 ml
1 1/2 cups unsalted butter - 375 ml
(at room temperature)

Combine the wine, shallots, pepper and wine vinegar in a saucepan. Bring to a boil over high heat. Reduce the heat and simmer for 25 minutes or until reduced to slightly more than 1/3 cup. If the reduction happens too quickly, add a little water during the process.

The butter should be cool enough to hold a finger imprint, but not of a soft melting consistency. Cut or gather the butter with your hand into 1/2- oz. pieces, about 1 tbsp. each.

Over low heat, add the cream to the lukewarm wine mixture. Add the butter, piece by piece (the second just before the first has completely disappeared and so on). Beat rapidly after each addition with a wire whisk. Continue adding butter and beating over low heat in this manner until all the butter has been added.

Hold the sauce in a double boiler with warm water in the bottom pan. When ready to serve, again place the sauce over low heat, and beat with a wire whisk until hot. Serve immediately. Serves 6.

Cider *Beurre Blanc*

Follow the directions for *beurre blanc*, substituting 1 cup of sweet cider for the white wine and reducing the amount of white wine vinegar to 1/4 cup. Serves 6.

Beurre Rouge

1 cup dry red wine - 250 ml
4 to 5 large shallots, peeled and diced
1/2 tsp. white pepper - 2 ml
1/2 cup vegetable stock - 125 ml
1 1/2 cups butter at room temperature - 375 ml

Follow the directions for *beurre blanc*, substituting vegetable stock for the white wine vinegar and red wine for white wine. Serves 6.

Tomato *Beurre Blanc*

The tomato is the variation in this sauce but you can add any type of vegetable you wish to a *beurre blanc*.

1 lb. ripe tomatoes - 454 g
2 tbsp. oil - 30 ml
salt
pepper, freshly ground
1/8 tsp.thyme - 0.5 ml
1 tbsp. finely chopped shallots - 15 ml
2 tbsp. dry white wine - 30 ml
2 tbsp. white wine vinegar - 30 ml
1 1/2 tbsp. crème fraîche - 23 ml
1/2 cup unsalted butter, at room temperature - 125ml

Blanch the tomatoes by placing them in a pot of boiling water for 10 seconds. Drain, stem, peel, halve and seed the tomatoes by cutting them in half horizontally and squeezing out the seeds. Dice. Heat the oil in a small skillet, add the diced tomatoes and sauté them over moderately high heat, stirring until thick and well reduced, for about 8 minutes. Season with salt, pepper and thyme.

Add the shallots, white wine and wine vinegar to 1 1/2-quart (6-cup) non-aluminum saucepan. Bring to a boil and cook until the mixture reduces to a glaze. Whisk in the *crème fraîche* over medium-high heat. Quickly reduce the cream mixture to half its volume. Add the butter which has been cut into 8 pieces, one at a time. When the second and subsequent pieces have all but melted, whisk constantly over medium heat. The object is to achieve a thick, creamy sauce. Remove from the heat. Pour or strain the sauce into the tomato mixture. Set in a warm place until ready to use. Serves 6.

Grapefruit Sauce

This delightful sauce complements both fish and chicken and can be used as a healthy dip.

1 cup thick mayonnaise - 250 ml
1/4 cup fresh cream - 60 ml
salt and pepper
1/2 cup chopped spinach leaves - 125 ml
1/4 cup chopped parsley - 60 ml
1/2 grapefruit, juice only
1 grapefruit, in sections for decoration
1 tomato, peeled and cut into cubes

Mix the mayonnaise (see the recipe in this chapter) with the cream, grapefruit juice, washed spinach leaves and parsley. Blend together in a food processor.

Pour the sauce onto a cold plate. Centre a slice of chilled pâté in the sauce and decorate the dish with tomato cubes and grapefruit sections. Refrigerate at least overnight before serving. Yields 1 1/2 cups of sauce.

Hollandaise Sauce

Classic sauce which everyone should know how to make. Hollandaise is an imperative in cuisine. Some of the chefs use it to thicken sauces, for *gratin* dishes or simply as an accompaniment for fish or vegetables.

1 tsp. white peppercorns, crushed - 5 ml
1 tbsp. white wine vinegar - 15 ml
3 egg yolks
1 cup melted butter - 250 ml
juice of 1/2 lemon
salt
water

In a shallow saucepan, mix together 2 tbsp. of water, the crushed peppercorns and the white wine vinegar. Set the pan over high heat and reduce the mixture by two-thirds.

Remove the pan from the heat. Whisking continuously, beat in 1 tbsp. of water and the egg yolks. Place the pan over very low direct heat or in a *bain-marie* (double boiler) filled with very hot but not boiling water.

Continue beating, making sure that the whisk reaches right to the bottom of the pan so that the egg yolks emulsify and do not begin to scramble. After 8 to 10 minutes, the mixture should be very creamy. Take great care that the temperature never exceeds 140°F(60°C).

Whisking continuously, gradually beat in the melted butter. If the sauce becomes too thick, add 1 or 2 tbsp. of lukewarm water; continue to whisk in the butter. Season to taste, then add a few drops of strained lemon juice. Strain the sauce through a muslin cloth if a very smooth consistency is desired. Serve at once, or keep the sauce in a *bain-marie* filled with warm water.

Mousseline Sauce

At the last moment add 4 to 6 tbsp. of whipped double cream to the Hollandaise sauce (about 1/3 part cream to 1 part sauce). Serve with poached vegetables such as broccoli, asparagus, courgettes or cauliflower.

Cooked Marinade

A versatile marinade that tenderizes various meats and enhances their flavour.

2 carrots
2 onions
1 celery stalk
2 tbsp. butter - 30 ml
4 cups full-bodied red wine - 1 L
1/2 cup red wine vinegar - 125 ml
3 cups water - 750 ml
1 bouquet garni
1 sprig rosemary
2 cloves
1 pinch peppercorns

Finely slice the vegetables, put in a large saucepan and sweat them in the butter. Add all the other marinade ingredients. Bring to a boil and then simmer for 20 minutes. Set aside to cool.

When the marinade is cold, add the meat and let it rest for 1 to 3 days. However, if you are going to serve the meat on the same day, add it while the marinade is still warm. Strain the marinade and reserve to use as the base for the sauce to accompany the meat. Yields 7 1/2 cups (for large pieces of meat or game).

Light Uncooked Marinade

This is suitable for small game, poultry, small fish and small pieces of meat which you intend to cook (especially to grill) the same day. The meat or fish should be placed in the marinade and turned from time to time. Ideal for use prior to barbecuing.

2 lemons, peeled and sliced
1 carrot, finely sliced
1 onion, finely sliced
4 tbsp. peanut oil - 60 ml
6 coriander seeds, coarsely crushed
1/2 cup dry white wine - 125 ml
salt
pepper, coarsely ground

Mix all the ingredients together. Add the lemon, carrot and onion slices. Pour over the meat or fish. Leave in the marinade for 3 to 4 hours. Yields 3/4 cup, or for 6 small portions.

Mayonnaise

A very basic and useful sauce from which many interesting variations can be prepared.

2 egg yolks
1/4 tsp. salt - 1 ml
1 tbsp. Dijon mustard - 15 ml
2 cups mild-flavoured oil, safflower - 500 ml
1 tbsp. lemon juice or wine vinegar - 15 ml
pepper, freshly ground, to taste

Combine the egg yolks, salt, pepper and mustard in a mixing bowl. Whisk them together. Slowly add the oil, whisking continually. Continue adding the oil, but more quickly as the volume increases. After whisking in all of the oil, add the lemon juice. Taste, and adjust the seasonings as desired. Yields 2 cups.

Mayonnaise Légère
1/3 cup whipped cream - 80 ml
1 cup mayonnaise - 250 ml

Fold the whipped cream into the mayonnaise. Chill and use as needed, mostly with fish terrines or cold fish.

Mayonnaise Cresson
1 tbsp. minced watercress - 15 ml
1 or 2 tsp. watercress juice - 5-10 ml
1 cup mayonnaise - 250 ml
1/3 cup whipped cream - 80 ml

To make watercress juice, purée the watercress in a food processor. Transfer to a kitchen towel or double thickness of cheesecloth and squeeze to extract the juice. Stir the watercress and the watercress juice into the mayonnaise. Fold in the whipped cream. Chill and use as needed, mostly with cold fish or fish pâté.

Mayonnaise (by hand)

6 egg yolks
1 tbsp. Dijon mustard - 15 ml
salt and pepper
3 tbsp. hot vinegar - 45 ml
1 quart peanut oil - 1 L

Separate eggs. Place yolks and all other ingredients except oil in a large bowl. Stir vigorously with a whisk. Add oil very slowly until proper consistency is reached. Yields: 5 cups.

EGG
DISHES

Eggs *Bordelaise*

2 eggs
1/2 cup chopped shallots - 125 ml
1/2 cup julienne of leeks - 125 ml
1/2 cup julienne of carrots - 125 ml
1/2 lb. spinach leaves - 227 g
1/3 cup baby mushrooms - 80 ml
1 tbsp. white vinegar - 15 ml
l tbsp. butter - 15 ml
1 tbsp. oil - 15 ml
2 oz. red wine
beurre rouge

Sauté the julienne of leeks and carrots and the spinach in the oil and butter. Sauté the baby mushrooms separately, and add them to the other vegetables. Poach the eggs in boiling salted water with the vinegar and 2 oz. (1/4 cup) of red wine. Once the eggs are cooked, place them on top of the sautéed vegetables. Prepare the *beurre rouge* in the same manner as *beurre blanc* and season it to taste. Glaze the eggs with the sauce and serve immediately. Serves 1.

Beurre Rouge
1 shallot chopped
2 oz. red wine - 60 ml
1 tbsp. fresh thyme - 15 ml
white pepper
1/3 cup unsalted butter - 80 g

Follow the recipe for *beurre blanc* in the chapter on Sauces, but substitute red wine for white wine.

Oeufs Caroline

6 eggs
4 oz. puff pastry, or
5 oz. short pastry
1 pinch flour
1 1/2 cups sweet corn - 375 ml
3 tbsp. butter - 45 ml
3 tbsp. white wine vinegar - 45 ml
1 tbsp. snipped chives - 15 ml
salt
white pepper, freshly ground
Hollandaise Sauce

The pastry cases

Roll out the puff pastry or short pastry on a lightly floured marble or wooden surface. Short pastry should be 1/10 inch thick; puff pastry should be rolled as thinly as possible, 1/8 inch.

Using a plain or fluted 3 1/4-inch pastry cutter, cut out 6 rounds of pastry. Line 6 tartlet tins, each 3 inches in diameter, with the pastry circles and flute the edges by pinching with your fingers. Prick the bottom of the pastry cases with a fork or sharp knife. Bake the pastry cases, unfilled, as follows.

Preheat the oven to 375°F(190°C). Place a circle of waxed paper in each pastry case and fill with dried beans. Bake in the preheated oven for 10 minutes. When the pastry shells are cooked, remove the beans and waxed paper. Remove the pastry shells from the tins and place on a wire rack to cool.

The eggs

Fill a shallow pan with water. Bring to a boil. Add the vinegar and poach the eggs. Remove them from the pan with a slotted spoon and put them into a bowl of very cold water. Cut off any ragged edges from the whites and place the eggs on a tea towel.

To assemble: preheat the broiler to high. In a saucepan, sweat the sweet corn with the butter and add the snipped chives. Cover the bottom of each pastry shell with corn and pour a little Hollandaise sauce (see the recipe in Sauces). Heat the poached eggs in boiling, salted water for 30 seconds. Drain well. Place an egg in each pastry shell. Pour a generous amount of sauce over and around the eggs. Place under a hot broiler for a few seconds until the sauce is a pale, nut-brown colour. Heat 6 plates until very hot and serve the eggs immediately. Cooking time is 4 minutes. Serves 4.

Oeufs Froids Carême

4 globe artichokes
juice of 1/2 lemon
6 tbsp. white wine vinegar - 90 ml
1 tbsp. flour - 15 ml
4 eggs
6 oz. smoked salmon, 4 medium-sized slices - 150 g
1/4 cup fish aspic (optional) - 60 ml
1 small truffle, about 1 oz. - 30 g
1/3 cup mayonnaise - 75 ml
1 tbsp. tomato ketchup - 15 ml
1 tsp. cognac - 5 ml
salt
pepper, freshly ground

Snap off the stalks of the artichokes and using a sharp knife, trim off the leaves until only the neatly shaped hearts are left. Sprinkle with lemon juice.

Cook the artichoke hearts in a saucepan of boiling, salted water with 3 tbsp. of vinegar, or in a white *court bouillon* (1 tbsp. flour, 3 tbsp. vinegar and water). They will take 20 to 35 minutes, depending on their size. Use the point of a knife to test when the artichokes are cooked, then leave them to cool in their cooking liquid.

Bring a shallow pan of water to the boil, add 1 tbsp. vinegar and poach the eggs. Lift them out with a slotted spoon and place in a bowl of very cold water. Trim the ragged edges from the whites and place the eggs on a tea towel.

Use a plain 3 1/4-in. pastry cutter to cut a neat circle from each slice of smoked salmon. Coat each with half-set fish aspic (see the recipe in the chapter on Soups). Decorate as you like with a little truffle. (Truffles *are* available at some specialty food stores and they are expensive, so they can be substituted with fresh chanterelle, boletus or oyster mushrooms.) Refrigerate the smoked salmon circles. Cut the trimmings into a small dice and set aside in a bowl.

To garnish, roughly chop the remaining truffle and add it to the diced salmon. Stir in the mayonnaise, ketchup and cognac and season to taste with salt and pepper. Keep refrigerated.

To serve, remove the chokes from the artichokes and pat the hearts dry with a cloth. Divide the garnish between the 4 artichoke hearts. Place an egg on each one and top with a round of smoked salmon. Serve on a cold plate. A sprig of chervil can be added for colour instead of the truffle. Serves 4.

Omelette à l'Oseille
Sorrel Omelet

A refreshing dish that tastes just as good cold as hot. If served cold, do not add the cream and gruyère cheese. Sorrel is a herb which we always seem to overlook, but if you use it properly, you can create magnificent results. This *omelette* is a fine example.

6 eggs
3/4 cup sorrel - 180 ml
3 tbsp. butter - 45 ml
1/2 cup double cream - 125 ml
1 pinch nutmeg
1 tsp. oil - 5 ml
1 tbsp. gruyère cheese, grated - 15 ml
salt
pepper, freshly ground

Preheat the broiler to high. Remove the stalks wash the leaves of the sorrel. Roll them up like a cigar and snip them very finely. Sweat in a sauté pan with 1 tbsp. butter until all the water from the sorrel has evaporated. Set aside.

Whip the cream in a bowl until the whisk leaves a trail when lifted. Season with salt and nutmeg. Set aside.

Break the eggs into a bowl and beat them with a fork. Season to taste with salt and pepper.

In an omelet pan, heat the oil with 2 tbsp. butter until the butter bubbles. Pour in the eggs, stirring very gently with a fork, and cook until set as you like it. Just before folding the omelet, spread the sorrel over the egg.

To serve, roll the omelet onto a silver or flameproof porcelain serving plate. Cover with the cream and sprinkle with the grated gruyère. Glaze immediately under the hot broiler for about 2 or 3 minutes, just long enough for the omelet to turn a pale golden colour. Serves 2.

Vegetable Omelet

3 eggs
1/2 cup julienne of carrot - 125 ml
1/2 cup julienne of zucchini - 125 ml
1/2 cup julienne of snow peas - 125 ml
1 tbsp. tomato cubes - 15 ml
fresh thyme for garnish
2 tbsp. butter - 30 ml
2 tbsp. oil - 30 ml
salt and pepper

Sauté the julienne of vegetables in butter for a few minutes, making sure they are nice and moist. Break the eggs in mixing bowl, add salt and pepper to taste. Prepare the omelet with beaten eggs to which the julienne of vegetables has been added and fold gently in, avoiding coloration of the bottom of the frying pan. Place the omelet on a plate. Surround it with *beurre blanc* (see the recipe in chapter on Sauces) and garnish the top with tomato cubes and fresh thyme. Serves 1.

Nova Scotia Lobster Omelet

3 eggs, extra large
1 cooked lobster, small
2 tbsp. tomato, cut into cubes - 30 ml
1/2 cup julienne of leeks, blanched - 125 ml
2 tbsp. oil - 30 ml
2 tbsp. butter 30 ml
salt and pepper
1 sheet parchment paper

Cut the cooked, shelled lobster into cubes and heat slightly in *beurre blanc* (see the recipe in the chapter on Sauces), reserving half the tail for presentation. Break the eggs into a mixing bowl and add salt and pepper to taste.

Heat the oil and butter in a frying pan and add the prepared eggs. Cook the omelet. Before rolling it, add the lobster, tomato cubes and leeks. Place the rolled omelet on parchment paper that has been lightly greased. Fold the parchment *en papillote* so it is sealed. Run the *papillote* under the broiler, just enough to colour the top. Cut the parchment lengthwise. Remove the omelet from the parchment, or leave it if you wish. Garnish with the half lobster tail. Glaze lightly with *beurre blanc*. Serve immediately on an oval plate. Serves 1.

ENTREES

Country-style Pâté

A simple pâté that can become a more elegant and extravagant terrine with the addition of goose liver, truffles, pigeon breast or duck breast. The chicken livers can be replaced by pork livers. Allow five to six days to marinate the meats for this pâté and an additional 24 hours of chilled storage prior to serving.

1/8 lb. salt pork - 57 g
1/2 lb. pork shoulder - 227 g
2/3 lb. pork fatback - 302 g
3 chicken livers
1/2 shallot, minced
1/2 tbsp. salt - 7 ml
1/2 tsp. pepper, freshly ground - 2 ml
1/2 tsp. allspice - 2 ml
a pinch of thyme
1/4 cup Madeira - 60 ml
1/8 cup cognac - 30 ml
1/2 bay leaf

Cut the salt pork, pork shoulder and 1/2 lb. of the fatback into 1/2-inch cubes. Clean the chicken livers and add them to the pork in a glass or ceramic bowl. In a small bowl, combine the shallot, salt, pepper, allspice, thyme, Madeira and cognac. Pour over the meat and stir well. Marinate for five or six days in the refrigerator.

Preheat the oven to 350°F (175°C).

Using the medium disk of a meat grinder, grind the meat mixture. Mix well with any remaining marinade. Reserve.

Slice the remaining fatback into very thin slices and line a 6-cup pâté mold or terrine, leaving a slight overhang. Pat the marinated forcemeat into the mold and place the bay leaf on top. Fold back the overhang of fatback. Cover with buttered foil, buttered side down.

Set the mold in a *bain-marie* in the oven and bake for approximately 75 minutes. Check for doneness by inserting a skewer into the centre of the pâté and leaving it there for 1 minute; then remove the skewer and carefully touch it to your lower lip. It should feel very hot. The melted fat and juices around the pâté should be clear. Remove the pâté from the oven when cooked. Cool to room temperature and chill for at least 24 hours.

For the presentation, unmold the pâté onto a serving platter. Slice a few slices and overlap them. Garnish with *cornichons* (small gherkins). Serves 6.

Duck Liver Mosaic with Wild Forest Pick and Little Orchard Fritters

This dish was a great success at The Grand in Halifax.

1 fresh duck liver, large (10 to 14 oz.) - 248-347 g
2 tsp. white pepper - 10 ml
1 tbsp. salt - 15 ml
2 tsp. sugar - 10 ml
2 tbsp. Armagnac - 30 ml
2 tbsp. port wine - 30 ml

Mushroom selection
1/2 cup truffles - 125 ml
1/2 cup fresh morels - 125 ml
1/2 cup fresh chanterelles - 125 ml

Duck liver preparation
Soak the duck liver in cold water for 3 hours. Open each lobe, gently breaking them. Remove the blood vessels from each and place the liver in a terrine. Mix the spices, Armagnac and port and pour over the liver. Set the liver in the marinade aside for 10 hours.

Trim and wash the mushrooms (with the exception of truffles, if they are preserved and not fresh). Lay them on a towel to dry and dust with salt and pepper.

Remove the liver and marinade after 10 hours. The liver will be very fragile. Gently press it down in an oven-proof terrine, layering with the mixed mushrooms. Cook in a *bain-marie* for 20 minutes at 350°F

(175 °C). Once baked, immediately place the terrine in the refrigerator with a weight on top. Serves 4.

Little Orchard Fritters

2 firm MacIntosh apples, peeled, cored and cut in sections
3 tbsp. fresh thyme - 45 ml
3 tbsp. fresh rosemary - 45 ml
3 tbsp. fresh chervil - 45 ml

Fritter batter

4 cups cooking oil for frying - 1 L
2 cups of beer - 475 ml
1 3/4 cups pastry flour - 430 ml
1/4 cup baking powder - 60 ml
salt and pepper to taste 1/2 cup olive oil - 125 ml

In a medium bowl, mix the beer, baking powder and flour and whisk vigorously. Peel and cut the apples. Put them in the olive oil to marinate. Heat the cooking oil for 5 minutes.

Once the fritter batter is thoroughly combined, remove the apples from the olive oil and dip them in the frying batter. Place gently in the hot oil. Cook until they are golden in colour. Once fried, dry them on paper towel and roll each fritter individually in chopped herbs.

To assemble for presentation, slice the baked duck liver mosaic with a warmed knife previously dipped in hot water. Arrange the fritters among the duck liver slices and serve with grilled bread. Serves 4.

Feuilleté of Snails in Red Wine Sauce

6 oz. puff pastry - 170 g
1 egg, beaten
20 snails
4 oz. goose liver - 125 g
3 shallots, chopped
1 lb. fresh spinach - 454 g
truffle juice

Lightly flour a table for the *feuilletage*, following the classic manner of making puff pastry (see the recipe in the Desserts chapter). With a large knife, cut the pastry in precise lines forming rectangles with a basic size of 6 inches by 9 inches. Again, cut the individual portions in order to make 4 small rectangles. Bake in a hot oven at 475 °F(246 °C) for 12 to 15 minutes.

Snail sauce
1/4 cup butter - 60 ml
1/4 cup red wine - 60 ml
1 tbsp. *fond de veau* (veal stock) - 15 ml
2 cups cream - 475 ml
salt and pepper to taste

Strain the liquid from the snails. Sauté the snails rapidly in a spoonful of the butter. Add the chopped shallots and sauté for a few minutes. Add the red wine, veal stock and seasoning. Add the truffle juice and cream. Remove the snails and let the sauce reduce until it coats the back of a spoon. Strain the sauce. Sauté the spinach separately, then strain it.

Cut the cooked puff pastry rectangles in halves. Gently place the spinach on the bottom halves, add the snails and cover them with a touch of the sauce. Gently put in place the tops of the *feuilletés*, or pastry rectangles and serve immediately. Serves 4.

Finnan Haddie

2 pieces of Finnan Haddie, 4 oz. each - 2-125 g
2 poached eggs
1 cup fish stock - 250 ml
1 handful spinach
1 leek, white part only
2 tbsp. butter - 30 ml

Bring the fish stock to a boil and poach the fish pieces for a few minutes. Poach two eggs in the usual manner so the yolks stay soft.

In a small saucepan, heat the 2 tbsp. of butter. Add the sliced leek and spinach. Let simmer for a few minutes and then pour the sauce onto the bottom of a plate. Place the finnan haddie on top of the vegetables. Place the poached eggs in the centre and surround with *beurre blanc* (see the recipe in the chapter on Sauces) and serve immediately. Serves 2.

Scallop Terrine with Saffron and Spinach

I have experienced everything with scallops — souf-flés, terrines, mousses, puff pastry, pan frying, steam-ing. This elegant cold *entrée* is one of the many ways to be creative with scallops.

1/2 cup fresh spinach, stemmed - 125 ml
1/2 tbsp. chopped fresh tarragon - 7 ml,
or 1/2 tsp. dried tarragon leaves, crumbled - 2 ml
1 tbsp. chopped fresh chervil - 15 ml,
or 1/4 tsp. dried chervil, crumbled - 1 ml
1 1/8 cups heavy cream, chilled - 280 ml
1/8 tsp. powdered saffron - .5 ml
1/8 lb. skinned salmon fillet, cooked - 63 g
1/2 lb. sea scallops, rinsed, patted dry,
chilled - 227 g
2 eggs
few hot red pepper sauce
pinch nutmeg
freshly grated white pepper, freshly ground
1/2 tbsp. unsalted butter, softened - 7 ml

Rinse the spinach with lukewarm water to remove all the sand and grit. Drain briefly; transfer to medium-sized skillet. Cover and cook over medium heat until the liquid boils. Uncover and boil, stirring, until al-most all of the liquid evaporates (for about 4 minutes). Transfer the spinach to a food processor or blender and add the tarragon and chervil. Process to a smooth purée. Transfer to a small bowl and refrigerate, covered, until chilled.

Combine 1/4 cup of the heavy cream and the saffron in a small saucepan. Slowly heat to a simmer and stir until the saffron is dissolved (for about 2 minutes). Pour the saffron mixture into a separate small bowl. Refrigerate, covered, until chilled.

Process the scallops in a food processor until minced. Stop the motor occasionally and scrape down the sides of the work bowl. Add the eggs, salt, hot red pepper sauce, nutmeg and white pepper to taste.

With the motor running, add 1 cup of the heavy cream in a thin stream within 30 seconds. Process for ·another 30 seconds. Remove the work bowl from the base, cover with plastic wrap and secure with an elastic band. Refrigerate for 30 minutes.

Return the work bowl to food processor base. With the motor running, add 1/4 cup of the heavy cream in a thin stream within 20 seconds. Taste the mixture for seasoning and adjust if necessary, remembering that the terrine will be served cold and the flavours will be muted. Remove half of the scallop mixture to small bowl and refrigerate, covered.

Preheat the oven to 350°F(175°C). Using the 1/2 tbsp. of softened unsalted butter, butter a 6-cup terrine.

With the food processor motor running, add the remaining 1/8 cup of heavy cream to the scallop mixture in the work bowl in a thin stream within 15 seconds. Deflate the mixture with 6 to 7 half-second pulses. Spoon half of the scallop mixture into the prepared terrine and smooth the top with rubber spatula. Transfer the remaining mixture to clean small bowl and refrigerate, covered.

Remove half of the previously refrigerated scallop mixture to a clean processor work bowl. With the motor running, add chilled saffron mixture in a thin stream within 25 seconds. Scrape down the sides of the work bowl. Process only long enough to create an even-coloured mixture. Deflate the mixture with 6 or 7 half-second pulses.

Remove the cooked salmon from the refrigerator and flake into small pieces. Remove and discard any bone. Scatter one-third of the salmon pieces over the scallop mixture in the terrine. Spoon the saffron-scallop mixture over the salmon and smooth the top with a rubber spatula.

Wash the processor work bowl thoroughly. Rinse under cold water and wipe dry. Return it to the base. Combine the reserved spinach and the remaining half of the previously refrigerated scallop mixture in the work bowl. Process until the spinach is evenly distributed.

Scatter half of the remaining salmon pieces over the saffron layer in the terrine. Spoon the remaining white scallop mixture over the salmon and smooth the top with a rubber spatula.

Scatter the remaining salmon over the scallop mixture in the terrine. Spoon the spinach mixture over the salmon and smooth the top with a rubber spatula. Rap the terrine sharply several times on a hard, flat surface to expel air bubbles. Cover the top loosely with buttered aluminum foil.

Place a large roasting pan in the oven, with or without a rack in the bottom of the pan. Place the filled terrine on the centre of the rack or in the centre of the pan. Pour enough warm water into the pan to come two-thirds up the sides of the terrine. Bake until a skewer inserted into the centre of the terrine withdraws clean, about 1 hour and 15 minutes. Cool, run a sharp knife around the sides of the terrine, unmold and serve. Serves 4 to 6.

Shrimp or Lobster Cocktail

This dish can be served throughout the year as an appetizer when it is finished with a rich cocktail sauce.

1 lb. baby shrimp, or lobster - 454 g
1/4 cup cognac - 60 ml
1/2 cup mayonnaise - 125 ml
1/2 cup ketchup - 125 ml
1/2 cup whipped cream - 125 ml
Boston lettuce, Belgian endive, tomatoes or hard-boiled sliced eggs

Marinate the shrimp or lobster in cognac for at least 10 minutes. Prepare the mayonnaise according to the recipe in the chapter on Sauces, then add ketchup to flavour the preparation. If desired, add some fresh whipped cream to lighten the sauce.

Dress in a cocktail glass or on a platter with such garnishes as Boston lettuce, Belgian endive, tomatoes or hard-boiled sliced eggs. Serve cold accompanied by warm, unbuttered toast. Serves 4.

Vegetable Pâté with Chicken Mousse

This beautiful pâté is made of fresh vegetables — which can be varied according to the season — lightly blanched and seasoned with a bit of salt, pepper and oil. The vegetables are combined and cooked with a mousse of chicken. The pâté should be served cold, in slices, surrounded by a tomato sauce.

Mousse
**3/4 lb. boneless chicken breast
(about 1 to 1 1/2 cups when cubed) - 375 ml
2 1/4 to 2 3/4 cups heavy cream - 560 to 685 ml
1/2 tsp. summer savory - 2 ml
1 tsp. tarragon - 5 ml
2 tbsp. fresh parsley, chopped - 30 ml
2 eggs
safflower oil
1 tsp. salt - 5 ml
1/2 tsp. pepper - 2 ml**

Texture is very important in this dish. The secret of getting it right is to trim the chicken carefully and to start with very cold ingredients and equipment. Remove all traces of fat from the chicken. Pull and scrape out the white tendons that run down the underside of each breast. Cube the chicken and place it in the bowl of a food processor, fitted with the metal blade. Refrigerate for about 1/2 hour. Prepare the vegetables while the chicken is chilling.

Remove the bowl from the refrigerator and place it on the base of the food processor. Add the summer savory, tarragon and parsley. Purée the mixture until smooth. With the machine running, add the chilled cream in a slow, constant stream. Check the mixture after adding 2 cups and add the remaining cream very slowly, just until the texture of whipped cream is achieved. The mixture should not be runny. Add the salt, pepper and set the mousse aside.

Vegetables

Any vegetables that are in season can be used. Have an eye for colours, which should contrast. The vegetables should be prepared and lightly blanched in boiling water, then removed with a slotted spoon to drain and dry on paper towels. When cool, they should be tossed gently with salt, pepper and a little oil and placed on a large plate or cookie sheet.

2 small zucchini (6 oz.) - 170 g
2 medium carrots (5 oz.) - 150 g
cauliflower (6 oz.) - 170 g
15 green beans (6 oz.) - 170 g
1 large tomato (10 oz.) - 280 ml

Prepare the vegetables by trimming the ends and cutting them into thin spears. Blanch the zucchini for 2 minutes, the carrots and cauliflower for 3 minutes and the green beans for 1 minute. The tomato need not be blanched but should be peeled, seeded and cut into strips.

Oil a 6-cup ovenproof glass loaf mold. Cover the bottom with a 1-inch deep layer of mousse. Arrange a layer of vegetables on top, alternating them with respect to colour and texture. Push the vegetables gently into the mousse. Cover with more mousse, then another layer of vegetables. Cover again with more mousse and vegetables, finishing the top with a layer of mousse. Cover with oiled parchment paper.

Place the mold in a slightly larger pan. Add water to the larger pan until it comes one-third of the way up the mold holding the mousse. Bake at 325°F (190°C) for 50 to 60 minutes. Let cool and refrigerate at least overnight before serving. Serve in slices, surrounded by the cold tomato sauce.

Sauce

1 tbsp. chopped shallots - 15 ml
4 tbsp. wine vinegar - 60 ml
1 tsp. tarragon - 5 ml
1 tbsp. tomato paste - 15 ml
1/3 cup water - 80 ml
2/3 cup tomato, peeled, seeded and diced - 180 ml
1 cup olive oil - 250 ml
(or 1/2 safflower and 1/2 olive, or to taste)
2 cups tomato juice - 500 ml
1 tsp. salt - 5 ml
1/2 tsp. pepper - 2 ml

Place the first 5 ingredients in a saucepan and reduce over high heat to about 1/3 cup. Cool slightly and place in a food processor with the metal blade. Add the diced tomato and purée until smooth. Add the oil and process for 20 seconds. Add the tomato juice and process for an additional 20 seconds. Season with salt and pepper if necessary. Serves 10.

FISH
AND
SEAFOOD

Pan-fried Halibut with *Beurre Blanc* and Sauerkraut

With this original approach, one can really personalize cuisine. Try to find a sauerkraut already prepared in white wine.

1 1/2 lbs. of halibut fillets or thin steaks - 902 g
1 tbsp. butter - 15 ml
1 tbsp. vegetable oil - 15 ml
flour for dusting
2 cups sauerkraut - 500 ml

Dust thin fillets or *escalopes* of halibut with flour. Melt the butter and oil in a hot frying pan. Sauté the fish until golden, adjusting the cooking time to the size of fish. Do not overcook.

Coat the dinner plates with tomato *beurre blanc* (see the recipe in the chapter on Sauces). Place the halibut on a bed of sauerkraut which has been simmered in vegetable stock, just to re-heat it. Serves 4 to 6.

Pan-fried Halibut with Cider *Beurre Blanc*

1 to 1 1/2 lbs. fresh halibut fillets - 454 to 680 g
1 tbsp. butter - 15 ml
1 tbsp. cooking oil - 15 ml

1/2 to 3/4 lb. spinach leaves - 227 to 350 g
2 apples, quartered and cored

Dust thin fillets or *escalopes* of halibut with flour. Melt the butter and oil in a hot frying pan. Sauté the fish until golden, adjusting the time to size of the fish. Do not overcook.

Coat the dinner plates with cider *beurre blanc* (see the recipe in the chapter on Sauces). Place the halibut on a bed of lightly sautéed spinach. Surround it with two quarters of scored, sautéed apples. Serves 4 to 6.

Poached Halibut
Beurre Rouge

1 1/2 lbs. fresh halibut fillets or thin steaks - 700 g
fish stock, or vegetable stock or court bouillon
1/2 to 3/4 lb. fresh spinach leaves - 230 to 340 g

Poach the halibut fillets or *escalopes* in fish stock and 1 cup of milk.

Coat the dinner plates with *beurre rouge* (see the recipe in the chapter on Sauces). Place the halibut on a bed of lightly sautéed spinach. Surround with sliced and lightly sautéed celery. Serves 4 to 6.

Striped Bass with Artichokes

These are two rare elements which go extremely well together. It is a dish which I recommend is served only in the summer months when the bass is freshly caught.

2 cooked artichokes
4 tbsp. artichoke cooking liquid - 60 ml
10 oz. striped bass fillets - 250 g
4 large or 8 small lobsters
1 small red pepper
6 leaves fresh basil
salt and pepper
a few drops of white wine
4 tbsp. butter, plus extra for the baking dish - 60 ml
1/2 cup heavy cream -125 ml

Trim the tops from 2 artichokes. Cut each bottom into 6 sections. Retain the cooking liquid for the sauce.

Cut the bass fillets diagonally so there are 4 pieces about equal in size. Place them between pieces of waxed paper and pound lightly with the flat side of a cleaver or a rolling pin to flatten slightly and to even the thickness. Twist off the lobster tails and remove the meat from the tail sections by cutting the ribbed underside with scissors and pulling away the shell so the meat remains in one piece.

Blanch the red pepper in boiling water for 5 minutes and peel. Remove the seeds and white parts of the pepper. Cut the pepper into fine julienne strips. Cut the basil leaves into fine strips. Butter a metal platter or shallow baking dish. Place the bass pieces on the dish, season with salt and pepper and sprinkle a few drops of white wine on the fillets. Dot the fish with 1 tbsp. of the butter.

Heat the oven to 525 °F(270 °C). Start the sauce by reducing the artichoke cooking liquid and cream in a heavy saucepan over high heat. When the sauce has reduced by half, turn the heat to low and whisk the remaining 3 tbsp. of butter into the sauce. Add red pepper and artichokes and warm over very low heat so that vegetables become warm but the sauce does not melt further. Just before serving add the basil and check the seasoning.

Put the fish in the preheated oven. It should cook for 3 minutes in all. After 1 minute, add the lobster tails to the platter and turn the pieces of fish. (The cooking time is for large lobster tails. Heat the smaller ones in the sauce at the same time you add the red pepper and artichokes, or sauté them separately over high heat for about 30 seconds until the flesh is firm.)

Serve on warm plates. Garnish each fillet with a lobster tail and spoon the vegetables and sauce over the fish. Serves 4.

Fillet of Sole in Champagne with Lobster Stuffing

1 Dover sole, trimmed
1 handful spinach, cleaned and washed
1/2 cup each julienne of leeks, carrots
and mushrooms - 125 g
1/4 cup whipping cream - 60 ml
salt and pepper
3 oz. lobster tail meat - 85 g
(cooked and cut into cubes)
2 oz. shallots - 50 g
1 1/2 cups champagne - 375 ml
beurre blanc

Prepare champagne *beurre blanc* (see the recipe in the chapter on Sauces), substituting champagne for the white wine and reserving some for poaching the fillets of sole. Barely sauté the julienne of leekss and carrots with the spinach leaves. This must stay crisp. Set aside.

Make a *duxelles* with the mushrooms and the whipping cream, salt and pepper and lobster cubes.

Duxelles de champignons
Clean and trim 4 oz. of mushrooms, or peelings and stalks, and chop them finely. Put them in a cloth and twist very tightly to extract all the liquid. Lightly brown half a chopped onion in butter. Add 2 chopped shallots, salt, pepper, nutmeg and the squeezed mushrooms. Stir over brisk heat until the mushrooms are cooked. Add the cooked lobster cubes. Chill and

keep in a cold place, covered with buttered paper.

Fillet the sole and poach the fillets in champagne for a few minutes. Remove and stuff the centre of the sole with the mushroom and lobster *duxelles*, reserving a little for garnish. Reduce the stock to half and add it to the champagne *beurre blanc*. Place the julienne of leeks and carrot and the spinach on the bottom of the plate. Arrange the fillets in the centre. Season the warmed *beurre blanc* and pour it over the sole. Top each fillet with a bit of reserved stuffing. Serves 1.

Fillet of Salmon
en Papillote

This is an original way to present many dishes. It can be served during the summer months, especially for an evening picnic.

4 fillets of raw salmon
1/2 lb. of fresh spinach, - 227 g
(washed and blanched)
1 cup vegetable julienne (leeks, carrots) - 250 ml
16 snow peas, blanched, for decoration only
1/4 cup white wine - 60 ml
salt and pepper to taste

Wrap all the ingredients in buttered parchment paper and cook in the oven for 20 minutes at 325 °F(165 °C). Parchments must rest on a bed of salt so that the paper doesn't burn.
Serve with *beurre blanc* in a side dish. Serves 4.

Beurre Blanc
1/2-3/4 cup unsalted butter - 125-180 ml
1/4 cup white wine - 60 ml
1/8 cup vinegar - 30 ml
1 tarragon leaf
2 parsley stalks
a few crushed white peppercorns
1/2 cup whipping cream - 125 ml
salt and pepper
lemon juice

In stainless steel pot, boil together the white wine, vinegar, herbs, tarragon, crushed parsley and white peppercorns. Let the mixture reduce until almost dry.

Add the cream and let reduce again until almost dry.

Beat the butter (at room temperature) until slightly foamy. Add seasonings and serve in a side dish with the salmon.

Grapefruit Salmon

1 3/4 lbs. fresh salmon fillets - 794 g
flour for dusting
2 pink grapefruit
1 lb. spinach - 454 g
1 tbsp. butter - 15 ml
1/4 cup consommé - 60 ml
beurre blanc

Fillet a fresh Atlantic salmon, making sure that all the bones are carefully removed. Allow about 7 oz. of salmon per serving.

Meanwhile, stem and wash the fresh spinach leaves. Peel the pink grapefruit and divide them into sections.

Dust the fillets lightly in flour. Pan-fry on a very high heat for a short time, turning once. Sauté the well-drained spinach in a very little bit of butter and the consommé.

Place a bed of spinach in the centre of the dinner plates. Top with salmon, surround it with grapefruit sections and a warm *beurre blanc* (see the recipe in the chapter on Sauces). Serves 4.

Nova Scotia Salmon Terrine

2 4-oz. fillets of salmon - 125 g each
dry sherry, enough to cover
basil, chervil, oregano, to taste
1 1/2 lbs. boneless fresh sole fillets - 680 g
1 egg white
1 medium-sized lobster tail
salt and pepper
2 cups fresh whipping cream - 500 ml
1/2 cup leeks julienne, white part only - 125 ml
1/2 cup carrot julienne - 125 ml
1/2 cup spinach leaves, blanched - 125 ml
1/4 cup pistachio nuts - 63 ml
1 cup cooked mushrooms - 250 ml
1 tbsp. freshly chopped parsley - 15 ml
1 1/2 cups fresh homemade mayonnaise - 375 ml
4 tbsp. fresh cream - 60 ml
1 tbsp. fresh chopped parsley - 15 ml
3 tbsp. lobster eggs (optional) - 45 ml

Marinate the salmon fillets in the sherry, basil, chervil and oregano for 24 hours in the refrigerator.

Mince the sole fillets in a food processor. Add the egg white and beat for a few seconds. Transfer the mixture to a chilled mixing bowl set in a bed of ice. Stir until very thick to produce a mousse and season to taste with salt and pepper. Add the lobster which has been cut into medium-sized chunks.

Sauté the julienne of leeks and carrot and the spinach leaves for a few seconds, but they must remain crisp. Slice the salmon into two layers, pat dry and place the julienne vegetables between the layers of salmon. Place a layer of the sole mousse mixture on the bottom of a lightly greased rectangular ovenproof glass baking dish (ensure that the dish is long enough to lay out the salmon fillets full length). Sprinkle with pistachio nuts and chopped parsley.

Lay a stuffed salmon fillet on the sole mousse and cover with another layer of mousse. Place another stuffed salmon fillet on the mousse and cover with the remaining mousse. Place the baking dish in a shallow pan of water and bake at 400°F(204°C) for 35 to 45 minutes. Remove from the oven and let cool. When cool, refrigerate for at least 24 hours before serving. Unmold the terrine by running the baking dish under hot water and/or running a knife around the edge of the mold.

In a blender mix the mayonnaise (see the recipe in the chapter on Sauces), fresh tarragon and parsley and the cream and mix until smooth. Season to taste. Transfer to a bowl and gently mix in the lobster eggs.

Pour a small amount of the mayonnaise sauce on a plate and place on it a slice of the terrine and garnish it with salad leaves or other colourful accompaniments. Serves 8.

Salmon and Caviar

If the salmon is sliced very thinly, it can even be eaten raw with the caviar. Also, the caviar could be used in a *beurre blanc*.

1 1/2 lbs. salmon fillet - 680 g
2 tbsp. caviar - 30 ml
1 lemon
2 tsp. butter - 10 ml
1/2 cup shallots - 125 ml
1 cup mushrooms - 250 ml
1/2-3/4 cup dry white wine - 125-180 ml
1 1/2 cups whipping cream - 375 ml
salt and pepper

Peel the lemon and chop the rind. Put it in a pan, cover with water and boil for 1 minute. When ready, strain and cool.

Clean the mushrooms. Season the salmon. Melt the butter in a pan. Add the chopped shallots. Cook for 6 minutes, then add the chopped mushrooms and cook for 6 more minutes. Add the salmon, 1/2 cup of water and the wine. Cook for 6 minutes. When the salmon is ready, take it out of the pan, put it on a dry cloth and with a sharp knife, take off the skin.

Deglaze the pan with the cream and boil for 2 minutes. Cut the salmon into 4 equal portions and place on a warm plate. Correct the sauce seasoning and pour it over the chopped lemon rind. Warm the sauce. Sprinkle the salmon with caviar and pour the sauce over. Serves 4.

Coarse Salt Salmon

1 lb. salmon fillet - 454 g
1 cup olive oil - 250 ml
2 tomatoes
1 carrot
1 cucumber
1 turnip
1 stalk fresh dill
1 stalk celery
1 squash
1/2 cup green beans - 125 ml
1 bouquet fresh basil
3 tbsp. coarse salt - 45 ml
salt and pepper

Peel the vegetables and cut them into sticks, 1 1/2 inches long and 1/4 inch wide. Cook one vegetable at a time in hot water. Place in ice water once cooked. Put all the vegetables in the top part of a steamer.

Peel and dice the tomatoes. Put them in a saucepan with the olive oil, basil, salt and pepper. Keep the tomato mixture warm.

Cut the salmon into 4 equal parts. Season and add to the vegetables in the steamer. Cook for 5 to 6 minutes. Arrange the vegetables on 4 plates and then add the salmon. Serve with coarse salt and the warm tomato sauce. Serves 4.

Salmon with Tomato *Beurre Blanc*

1 lb. centre-cut salmon - 454 g
butter, for greasing
salt
1/2 cup *crème fraîche* **-125 ml**
2 tbsp. Dijon mustard - 30 ml
spinach, for garnish

Cut 1/2-inch thick steaks of salmon. Grease a heavy baking sheet with butter. Arrange 4 salmon pieces on the sheet, about 3 to 4 inches apart. Sprinkle with salt.

Mix the *crème fraîche* with the mustard, combining well. Coat each portion of salmon with the mixture. Hold in the refrigerator until ready to cook.

Preheat the broiler for 15 minutes. Place the baking sheet about 4 inches from the broiler heat, keeping the door ajar. Broil for about 4 1/2 to 5 minutes until the salmon is just barely done and the creamy topping is spotted brown.

Spoon tomato *beurre blanc* (see the recipe in the chapter on Sauces) onto warmed plates and top with the salmon steaks. Garnish with spinach. Serve immediately. Serves 4.

Casserole of Maritime Scallops

An unusal and simple dish with an accent of fantasy created by the julienne of vegtables.

20 oz. scallops - 567 g
4 chopped shallots
4 oz. white wine - 60 ml
2 cups fresh cream - 500 ml
4 tbsp. butter - 60 ml

Julienne of vegetables
1/4 cup carrots - 60 ml
1/4 cup leeks - 60 ml
1/4 cup celery - 60 ml
1/4 cup zucchini - 60 ml
1/4 cup spinach leaves - 60 ml
1/4 cup peeled tomato cubes - 60 ml

Simmer the scallops, shallots, white wine, 2 tbsp. of butter and julienne of vegetables. Let boil for 2 minutes and then remove the seafood and garden julienne. Let the stock reduce with the cream until the sauce thickens. Whisk in another 2 tbsp. of butter until it melts.

Season to taste and serve this sauce with your dish of Digby scallops. To add a professional touch, top with a puff pastry *fleuron*. Serves 4.

Lobster *Batelière*

This is a wonderful *mélange* of classic and modern cuisine.

2 lobsters, about 1 1/2 lbs. each - 680 g each
2/3 cup chopped fresh mushrooms - 160 ml
3 tbsp. butter - 45 ml
3 tbsp. flour - 45 ml
1/4 tsp. salt - 1 ml
1/2 tsp. dry mustard - 2 ml
dash of paprika
1 1/2 cups milk - 375 ml
1/4 cup grated cheese 60 ml
3 tbsp. sherry, or
1 tbsp. lemon juice - 15 ml
2 tbsp. finely grated cheese - 30 ml

Fill a deep container with enough water to cover the lobster. For each quart (4 cups) of water add 1/4 cup of salt. Bring the water to a rapid boil. Then, grasping each lobster behind the head, plunge it into the water. Cover the container. Allow the water to return to a gentle boil. Cook the lobsters for 20 minutes from the time of plunging them into the water. If the lobsters are small (less than 1 lb.) 15 minutes of cooking time is sufficient. Cool the cooked lobsters quickly under cold water and drain them.

Remove the meat from the body and claws. Save the body shells. Cut the lobster meat into bite-sized pieces. Melt 1 tbsp. of the butter, add the mushrooms and pan-fry until tender. Melt the remaining butter in the top part of a double boiler. Stir in the flour and seasonings. Add the milk slowly and cook over hot water, stirring constantly until thickened. Stir in the 1/4 cup grated cheese and continue stirring until melted. Add the lobster, mushrooms and sherry or lemon juice. Mix well.

When thoroughly heated, spoon the mixture into the lobster shells arranged in a shallow baking dish. Sprinkle with finely grated cheese and broil 4 inches from the top heat for about 2 minutes or until the cheese is golden brown. Serves 4.

Moules à la Marinière

This is a dish which has been served for centuries, and if well prepared, it is an absolutely marvelous meal.

3 lbs. mussels - 2 L
1 medium-sized onion
7 tbsp. unsalted butter - 105 ml
2 tbsp. Dijon Mustard - 30 ml
1/2 cup dry white wine - 125 ml
3 sprigs parsley
pinch of freshly ground pepper

Scrub and clean the mussels. Chop the onion very finely. In a saucepan big enough to hold the mussels in their shells, cook the onion very slowly in 3 1/2 tbsp. of butter without letting it brown.

When the onion is transparent, which should take 15 to 20 minutes, add the Dijon mustard, moisten with the dry white wine, add the mussels, then the 3 sprigs of parsley, chopped, and a pinch of freshly ground pepper. Cover the saucepan tightly, place over high heat and let the mussels boil rapidly for a few minutes until they open.

Remove the mussels with a slotted spoon and keep them warm in a covered soup tureen. Pour the liquid into another saucepan. Be sure NOT to pour out the broth at the bottom of the pot, which will contain sand, despite careful cleaning. Boil to reduce the liquid by half if you like it strong; less, if you prefer a more delicate flavour. Add the remaining butter, then pour the liquid over the mussels, sprinkle a pinch of chopped parsley on top, and serve.

Moules à la marinière must be cooked at the last moment, and guests must wait for them. Mussels prepared in advance and kept warm will darken and dry out. Serves 4.

Moules Poulette
Mussels with Cream Sauce

This is a classic dish which I often prepare because of the great harvest of mussels we have in the Digby area.

2 tbsp. butter - 30 ml
3 tbsp. flour - 45 ml
1 cup heavy cream - 250 ml
salt and pepper (optional)

Cook as for *Moules à la Marinière* (see the preceding recipe and use the quantities described). Separate the shells, arranging the halves with the mussel attached, on dinner plates. Melt the 2 tbsp. of butter in a saucepan and mix in the 3 tbsp. of flour. Add the broth, leaving any sandy residue in the bottom. Bring to a boil, mixing with a whisk. Let it simmer for 2 minutes. Add 1 cup of heavy cream and bring to a boil again. Add salt and pepper, if needed. Cook for a few minutes and spoon the sauce over the mussels. Serves 4.

Scallops Jacqueline

Every year Digby has a Scallop Day, and Jacqueline was the Scallop Festival Queen in 1983. I developed this recipe for her then and it is still a great favourite on the menu at The Pines.

Bouillon
1/2 leeks
2 carrots
2 bay leaves
2 shallots
2 celery sticks
2 slices ginger root
salt and pepper
fresh herbs
12 cups water - 3 L

Prepare the bouillon with the water, leeks, celery, carrots and ginger root. Let simmer with some fresh herbs for at least 1/2 hour.

Wash the scallops well and place them above the stock for a basic steaming process in order to let the scallops infuse the flavour of the vegetables and the ginger fumes. Cover and let the scallops simmer gently through the steam for at least 3 or 4 minutes and season to taste. Please note that the seasoning is extremely important.

Garniture for the julienne
leeks, white part only
fresh herbs, thyme and rosemary (small bouquet)
olives

Prepare a julienne of leeks, white part only, and steam with scallops just before they are finished cooking. This process will only take a few seconds. Once cooked, cool off the julienne in ice water in order to keep the colour fresh.

For the presentation, place the scallops on a warm plate keeping an eye on the colour and place them in such a way as to create a harmonious arrangement. Pour a *cordon* (ribbon) of *beurre blanc* (see the recipe in the chapter on Sauces) around the scallops. Sprinkle the scallops with more julienne of leeks and the fresh herbs. Serves 4.

Scallops with Puff Pastry

This recipe has many variations. Scallops, lobsters, oysters, mussels, vegetables and even asparagus could be used.

12 large scallops
6 1/3 oz. puff pastry, fresh or frozen - 180 g
1 beaten egg, to brush on dough
1 tbsp. butter - 15 ml
1 1/3 cups heavy cream - 330 ml
salt and pepper
truffle juice

In a small shallow casserole or a saucepan, melt the butter, uncovered, for 2 minutes. Add 1 tbsp. of the truffle juice, the cream and salt and pepper. Boil gently for 3 to 4 minutes, or until the liquid has reduced by half. While the sauce is cooking, place the scallops in a small saucepan over medium heat and bring barely to a boil. Lower the heat, cover the pan, and simmer for 1 minute, then remove from the heat.

With a serrated knife, carefully cut 4 cooked puff pastry rectangles in halves. Place the bottom halves on hot plates or a serving platter. Lift the scallops out of their juice with a skimmer or slotted spoon and place three of them on each pastry. Pour the sauce over the scallops. Cover with the top half of each pastry, and serve immediately.

A delicious variation of this dish can be made using 8 scallops and 8 large oysters, instead of only scallops. Open the oysters and poach them in their juice for 30 seconds. Add their juice to the sauce as well as that of the scallops. Serves 4.

Scallops Baked in Shells

A *nouvelle cuisine* approach to scallops.

1 lb. scallops - 454 g
1/4 cup heavy cream - 60 ml
4 tsp. fine, dry bread crumbs - 20 ml
4 tsp. melted butter - 20 ml
salt and pepper

Separate the scallops and place 4 or 5 in each of 4 greased scallop shells or custard cups. Season with salt and pepper and add 1 tbsp. of cream to each shell or baking dish. Top each dish with 1 tsp. of bread crumbs and 1 tsp. of melted butter. Bake at 450°F(232°C) for about 20 minutes. Serves 4.

Warm Oyster *Feuilletés* with Raspberries

24 oysters
10 oz. puff pastry - 280 g
pinch of flour
1 egg yolk, beaten with 1 tsp. milk, to glaze
1/2 cup very fine French green beans or sea asparagus - 125 ml
1 cup bean sprouts - 250 ml
1/4 cup shallots - 60 ml
32 winkles (optional)
1 tsp. oil - 5 ml
3 tbsp. raspberry vinegar - 45 ml
1 tbsp. double cream - 15 ml
3/4 cup butter - 175 ml
1 cup fresh raspberries - 250 ml
salt

Puff pastry

On a lightly floured marble or wooden surface, roll out the pastry to a thickness of about 1/4 inch. (See the recipe for puff pastry in the chapter on Desserts.) Using a small sharp knife, cut out 4 oyster shapes. Place the pastry shapes on a flan tin or small baking sheet brushed with a little water. Brush the pastry shapes with a mixture of the egg yolk and milk and "pink" the edges with a knife. Lightly cut a line 1/10 inch from this edge (this will form the lid after baking). Leave the pastry to rest for at least 20 minutes in the refrigerator or in a cool place.

Meanwhile, preheat the oven to 425°F(220°C). Bake the pastry "oysters" in the preheated oven for 12 minutes. When they are cooked, cut around the line you drew earlier. Slip the knife blade underneath and lift off the lids. Set the pastry cases and their lids on a wire rack and keep them warm.

Open the oysters over a bowl so as to catch the juices. Keep the oysters on absorbent paper at room temperature and strain the juices into a shallow pan.

Top and tail the green beans and cut them into 1/2-inch lengths. Cook them in boiling, salted water until they are tender but still crisp. Slice into julienne strips, plunge them in ice water, drain and set aside.

Add the bean sprouts to boiling, salted water for 30 seconds, plunge them into ice water, drain and set aside.

Peel and finely chop the shallots.

Add the 1 tsp. of oil to a pan of boiling, salted water and cook the winkles for 2 minutes. Remove them from their shells with a pin.

To prepare the sauce, add the chopped shallots and raspberry vinegar to the pan containing the oyster juices. Rub one-third of the raspberries through a sieve into the pan. Set over high heat and reduce the liquid until syrupy. Add the cream and let the mixture bubble once more. Stir in the butter, a little at a time. Correct the seasoning if necessary, and keep the sauce warm.

To serve, preheat the oven to 375°F(190°C). Place the oyster-shaped pastry shells on serving plates and warm them in the oven for 30 seconds. Meanwhile, stir the beans, bean sprouts, oysters and winkles into the sauce. Set the pan over medium heat, and as soon as the sauce begins to tremble, take the pan off the heat.

Fill each pastry shell with 2 oysters, arrange 4 oysters around each one and pour the sauce into and around the pastry shells. Top each one with its lid. Arrange the remaining raspberries on the sauce around the edge of each plate and serve immediately. Serves 4.

Baked Atlantic Scallops

1 lb. scallops - 454 g
2 tbsp. salt - 10 ml
1/2 cup chopped onion - 125 ml
1 1/2 cups chopped celery - 375 ml
1 cup chopped mushrooms - 250 ml
1 cup chopped green pepper - 250 ml
6 tbsp. butter - 90 ml
1/4 cup flour - 60 ml
2 cups milk - 500 ml
1 cup soft bread crumbs - 250 ml
1 tbsp. melted butter - 15 ml
1/4 cup finely grated cheese - 60 ml

Separate the scallops and sprinkle them with 1 tsp. of the salt. Cook the onion, celery, mushrooms and green pepper in 2 tbsp. of the butter until tender. Make a cream sauce with the remaining 4 tbsp. of butter, the salt, flour and milk.

Combine the scallops, sautéed vegetables and cream sauce and place the mixture in a greased casserole. Combine the bread crumbs and butter and put them on top of the casserole. Sprinkle with grated cheese. Bake in a moderate oven, 375 °F(190 °C), for about 20 minutes. Serves 6.

MEAT
AND
POULTRY

Grenadins of Lamb stamped with Marrow, and Red Pepper Bisque

By invitation from Ocean Spray, I was invited to New York to attend an international gathering of chefs from France and the U.S. I prepared this dish for the main dinner of the exhibition.

3 lbs. lamb saddle - 1.4 kg
1/2 lb. bone marrow - 227
1/2 cup butter - 125 ml
2 tbsp. olive oil - 30 ml
fresh thyme, a small bouquet
2 tbsp. coarse salt - 30 ml
salt and pepper to taste
materials - 1 cutting board, 1 boning knife,
1 butcher's cleaver

Ask your local butcher to remove the bones from the saddle of lamb. Take only the top fillets. Cut the *grenadins*, or tender little slices of fillet, in approximately 2-oz. pieces and flatten them gently with the cleaver.

For the marrow preparation, use only centre-cut beef marrow bones. Ask the butcher to crack them or buy them already cracked. Add the coarse salt and thyme to boiling water and let it simmer for a few minutes. Blanch the marrow bones, lift them out to cool and remove the marrow from the bones. Place the marrow back in the liquid for less than 5 minutes then cool them again. Cut a slice of marrow for each slice of lamb fillet. Set these aside.

To cook the lamb *grenadins*, preheat a sauté pan over medium heat. Add the oil and butter. Brown the lamb well, but the insides should remain pink. Add salt and pepper to taste and set aside.

Tomato brouillade, or compote

1 lb. red tomatoes - 454 g
1 bouquet fresh basil
1/4 cup butter, room temperature - 60 ml
1 tbsp. olive oil - 15 ml
1/2 cup chopped shallots - 125 ml
1 large garlic clove
1 tbsp. tomato paste - 15 ml
fresh thyme, celery, small onions for cooking (a flavouring agent only)
salt and pepper to taste

Choose ripened tomatoes. Cut off the tops and plunge the tomatoes into boiling water to remove the skins; transfer them immediately to an ice bath. Drain, cut them in halves, press and remove the seeds. Place them in a food processor and process until chopped. Wash the basil leaves and reserve the best ones for garnishing. Process the remaining basil finely and set aside.

Preheat a saucepan with the butter and olive oil. Add the shallots and let them gently colour. Add the tomato paste, garlic, celery, pepper and chopped tomatoes. Let the mixture simmer for 40 minutes over low heat. Add the chopped basil and season to taste. Set aside.

Red Pepper Bisque
2 red peppers
1/4 cup olive oil - 60 ml
1/4 cup shallots - 60 ml
1/4 cup cream - 60 ml
1/2 cup butter, at room temperature - 125 ml
salt and pepper to taste

Skin the red peppers by plunging them in hot fat before peeling them. Bring the cream to a boil and add the red peppers. Add the olive oil and shallots and cook them gently on medium heat for 10 minutes. Season to taste and blend to a purée. Strain into a china cup and finish the sauce by adding the butter, piece by piece.

For the final assembling, centre the tomato *brouillade* on four plates. Arrange the lamb *grenadins* around the tomato and top each one with one slice of bone marrow. Distribute the red pepper sauce on each and serve immediately. Garnish with the reserved basil leaves. Serves 4.

Chicken Supreme with Mushroom Sauce

Mushroom Sauce
3 tbsp. butter - 45 ml
1/2 cup white wine - 125 ml
1 cup double cream - 250 ml
4 tbsp. butter - 125 ml
1 cup chicken stock - 250 ml
1/2 lb. small raw mushrooms - 227 g

Place the 3 tbsp. of butter and the white wine in a pan to reduce. Add the chicken stock and mushrooms. Bring to a boil and cook until the mushrooms are tender. Add the cream and reduce again until the sauce coats the back of a spoon. Add the second amount of butter (4 tbsp.) and strain the sauce. Add salt and pepper to taste.

Chicken
4 chicken breasts, skinned and boned
1 1/2 cups carrots, julienne - 375 ml
1 1/2 cups celery, julienne - 375 ml
1 1/2 cups green beans, cut in half - 375 ml
4 stalks of tarragon for garnish
salt and pepper

Season the chicken with salt and pepper. Steam, without allowing the chicken to touch the water, until it is tender. Put the vegetables and tarragon stalks under the chicken to form a cushion and steam for 4 to 5 minutes. Remove the tarragon stalks. Place the sauce on the plate and garnish each chicken breast with the vegetables. Serves 4.

Roast Leg of Lamb

A dish that is known worldwide, but this recipe is from the Annapolis Valley.

1 fresh leg of lamb, about 6 to 7 lbs. - 2.7 to 3.2 kg
1/3 lb. fresh chanterelle mushrooms - 150 g
6 slices white bread
1 small cucumber, peeled, seeded and finely diced
3/4 to 1 cup unsalted butter - 180 to 250 ml
1 tbsp. oil - 15 ml
salt
pepper
white peppercorns
1 bouquet fresh thyme, rosemary, chives and parsley
1 tbsp. Dijon mustard - 15 ml
2 tsp. butter - 30 ml

Bone the fresh lamb carefully to remove the whole bone without cutting the flesh from the outside. If this is too difficult, ask the butcher to bone the lamb. Trim the white bread and chop it in a food processor with the herbs. Process for a few minutes, just until blended.

Wash and trim the chanterelles and cut them into small pieces. In 2 soup-spoons of the butter, very rapidly sauté the mushrooms until all the juice evaporates. Add salt and pepper to taste. Strain the mushrooms, add the remaining butter to the same frying pan and sauté the breadcrumbs with the herbs and cucumbers. Add salt and pepper to taste. Once slightly coloured, mix the chanterelles with the herbs and remove quickly from the heat. Cool for a few minutes.

Meanwhile, preheat the oven to 450°F(230°C). Stuff the lamb with the breadcrumb mixture reserving some. Tie the leg of lamb with string to re-form the original shape of the leg.

Place the leg of lamb in the oven and roast it gently for at least 25 minutes, in 1 tbsp. of oil. Turn it often. The remaining herbs may be added to season the roast during cooking. Take the leg of lamb from the oven and remove the string. Brush the leg with the 2 tsp. of butter mixed with the Dijon mustard and peppercorns. Cover the leg with the remaining stuffing. Again place it in the oven at 250°F(120°C) for 10 minutes. Once cooked, let the meat rest.

Slice the lamb thinly and surround the slices with a bit of lamb juice. Top with *beurre noisette*, butter that has been cooked to a light hazelnut colour and kept very hot before adding to the juice of a lemon. Fresh herbs can be used to enhance the presentation. Serves 4 to 6.

Pot-au-Feu
Sweetbreads with Baby Spring Vegetables

For connoisseurs, this dish was a huge success at The Grand in Halifax.

Baby vegetables
4 spring carrots with green tips
4 spring baby beets with tips
4 spring cherry tomatoes
4 spring zucchini
4 spring green asparagus
4 spring shallots
a small handful chopped chives

Consommé preparation
1/2 lb. sweetbread, veal - 227 g
2 stalks celery
3 carrots, peeled
1 leek, white part only
2 onions, chopped and gently browned
thyme, bay leaf, bouquet garni
salt and pepper

Trim the veal sweetbreads after soaking them in cold water for at least 2 hours. Place in a large pot with fresh cold water to cover and add the celery, carrots, leek and onions. Let it simmer gently for at least 2 hours, making sure the stock does not boil.

Meanwhile, peel the baby vegetables, except the beets, and place them in a strainer in the simmering pot with the sweetbreads. Remove the baby vegetables when cooked, and set them aside. Gently remove the sweetbreads and cool immediately. Peel and cook the baby beets and set aside.

Correct the seasoning of the consommé and strain it through a piece of cheesecloth. Set aside and keep warm.

Arrange the baby vegetables in 4 large soup plates. Slice the sweetbreads and pan-fry them for a few seconds, just to colour both sides. Place them in the soup plates with the baby vegetables. Pour the consommé with the chopped herbs over the vegetables and the sweetbreads. Serves 4.

Author's Note: when preparing your *pot-au-feu*, you can also add a half chicken to increase the flavour of the broth. If you rarely make a broth or other *fumet*, you can add a cube of beef bouillon.

Rappie Pie, "Acadian Way"

You can't leave Nova Scotia without tasting Acadian gastronomy and Rappie Pie is a fine example.

5 or 6 lbs. fowl or chicken, quite fat - 2.5 kg
5 1/2 lbs. large peeled potatoes - 2.75 kg
2 medium-sized onions
salt and pepper

Cut the fowl into pieces. Cover with water and cook. Add finely chopped onions, salt and pepper. Peel, wash and grate the potatoes, noting how much you have after grating.

Squeeze the potatoes (in a bag, about 2 cups at a time) until they are quite dry. Pack in a bowl. When the potatoes are all squeezed, loosen them up in a large pan. Gradually add the boiling broth from the chicken, stirring slowly. If there is not enough broth, add boiling water until you have as much potato mixture as before they were squeezed. (If your chicken is not very fat, melt a piece of fat pork and add it to the potato mixture.) Add salt and pepper to taste.

Grease a 17-inch by 12-inch pan. Spread half of the potatoes into the pan. Distribute the chicken evenly over this, then cover with the other half of the potato mixture. Bake at 400°F(204°C) for 2 hours. Rappie Pie should be brown, crusty and delicious. Serves 5.

BISCUITS AND MUFFINS

Apple Muffins

A spontaneous creation after a journey to the Annapolis Valley.

1/2 cup margarine - 125 ml
1 cup sugar - 250 ml
pinch of salt
3 eggs
1 3/4 cups all-purpose flour - 430 ml
1 1/2 tsp. baking powder - 7 ml
5 tbsp. milk - 75 ml
1 cup apples, grated in a food processor - 250 ml

Cream the margarine, sugar and salt until light and fluffy. Add the eggs, one at a time, beating each in well. Sift the flour and baking powder and gradually add to the mixture, alternately with the milk. Lightly fold in the grated apple and turn the mixture into large muffin cups placed in deep muffin tins. Sprinkle with the streusel mixture and bake at 400 °F(205 °C) for about 20 minutes. Test for doneness with a toothpick. Yields 8 large muffins.

Streusel
1/2 cup unsalted butter, chilled - 125 ml
2/3 cup granulated sugar - 160 ml
1 3/4 cups all-purpose flour - 430 ml
1/2 tsp. vanilla extract - 2 ml
1 tsp. cinnamon - 5 ml

Combine all of the ingredients in a food processor until loose and crumbly.

Blueberry Muffins

What a great start to a day!

1/2 cup margarine - 125 ml
1 cup sugar - 250 ml
pinch of salt
3 eggs
1 3/4 cups all-purpose flour - 430 ml
1 1/2 tsp. baking powder - 7 ml
4 tbsp. milk - 60 ml
1 cup blueberries, fresh or frozen
(thawed and well drained) - 250 ml

Cream the margarine, sugar and salt until light and fluffy. Add the eggs, one at a time, beating each in well. Sift the flour and baking powder and gradually add to the mixture, alternately with the milk. Lightly fold the blueberries into the mixture and turn into large muffin cups placed in deep muffin tins. Bake at 400 °F(205 °C) for about 20 minutes. Test for doneness with a toothpick. Yields 8 large muffins.

Bran Muffins

A great muffin is as much appreciated as a glorious croissant.

3/4 cup whole wheat flour - 180 ml
2 tsp. baking powder - 10 ml
1/2 tsp. baking soda - 2 ml
1/2 cup margarine, - 125 ml or
1/4 cup butter, softened - 60 ml
1/2 cup brown sugar - 125 ml
2 extra large eggs
1/3 cup liquid honey - 80 ml
1 1/2 cups buttermilk (or as required) - 375 ml
2 cups bran - 500 ml
1/8 cup rolled oats - 30 ml
1/4 cup + 2 tbsp. broken dates - 90 ml
1/3 cup raisins - 80 ml
3/4 cup finely grated raw carrot - 180 ml

Cream the butter and sugar, then beat in the eggs and honey. Add the bran and rolled oats, alternately with buttermilk. Fold in the dry ingredients with the grated carrot, raisins and dates. Fill large muffin cups generously. Top with a garnish of a whole date, banana chip, whole walnut or pecan.

Bake at 400°F(205°C) for approximately 20 minutes. Test for doneness with a cake tester or toothpick. Yields 8 large muffins.

Tea Biscuits

A delicious biscuit that complements a meal. Or, to share these with your friends any time of day makes it a special occasion.

2 cups flour - 500 ml
4 tsp. baking powder - 20 ml
1 tbsp. sugar - 15 ml
1/2 tsp. salt - 2 ml
1/2 cup butter, chilled and cut into 12 pieces - 125 ml
1 egg
buttermilk, enough to equal 1 cup when added to the egg

Sift the flour, baking powder, sugar and salt together. Place in the bowl of a food processor. Add the butter pieces and blend to a coarse meal. Break the egg into a 1-cup measure. Add buttermilk to the egg, enough to bring the mixture to 1 cup. Mix with a fork. Add buttermilk-egg mixture to the dry ingredients in the food processor. Process only until a rough ball forms. *Do not* overprocess.

Remove the dough from the work bowl. Knead briefly on a pastry cloth dusted with flour. Roll to a thickness of 1 1/2 to 2 inches. Shape into 15 biscuits with a cutter. Place the biscuits on a greased baking sheet so that they are touching. Bake at 400°F(205°C) until golden brown. To enhance their colour, place a generous dab of butter on top of each tea biscuit before placing in the oven. Yields 15 tea biscuits.

Waffles

A good homemade waffle is a special treat.

1 3/4 cups sifted flour - 430 ml
2 cups milk - 500 ml
1/2 to 3/4 cup melted butter - 125 to 185 ml
8 egg yolks
6 egg whites, stiffly beaten
3 tbsp. sugar - 45 ml
pinch of salt
pinch of yeast

Mix the flour, salt, yeast and sugar in a bowl. Gradually moisten with the milk and the egg yolks. Incorporate the melted butter and the stiffly beaten egg whites into the mixture.

After heating the waffle iron, grease the inside. Gradually pour in enough batter to just cover the surface. Close the waffle machine and tilt it so that the batter evenly covers the two surfaces of the waffle iron. This ensures a crispy waffle.

Accompany waffles with sifted icing sugar and garnish with whipped cream or with tasty homemade jams and preserves. Yields 10 waffles.

DESSERTS

Crème Anglaise
Custard Cream

This traditional English custard can be transformed, in modern ways, for use in many inspired creations.

4 cups milk - 1 L
8 egg yolks, beaten
1 1/4 cups sugar - 310 ml
2 whole vanilla beans
ice water

While a cake or other desserts chill, make the *crème anglaise*. Bring the milk to a boil in a medium-sized saucepan. Mix the egg yolks and sugar in a bowl and whisk the hot milk into the mixture. Return it to the saucepan, add the vanilla beans and stir over low heat until the custard coats the back of a spoon, for about 10 minutes. Do not allow it to boil or it will curdle. Immediately place the *crème anglaise* in a bowl and set it in a pan of ice water to cool. Stir occasionally. When it is cool, remove the vanilla beans. Yields 4 cups.

Crème Fraîche

A naturally fermented, marvelously thick cream. This is found in its true form only in France. Sour cream can't be used as a substitute, but this recipe produces a reasonable facsimile. It is not used to thicken sauces, but to change their texture. Don't rush the fermenting process.

2 cups heavy cream - 500 ml
1/3 cup buttermilk - 80 ml

Combine the cream and buttermilk in a saucepan and heat until it is warm (just under 100°F(38°C)). *Do not* let it get hot; this would kill the bacteria cultures in the buttermilk.

Pour the mixture into a plastic or glass container. Place the container, covered, in a basin of warm water, 100°F(38°C).

Allow it to stand for 12 to 36 hours, or until thick. Every now and then, replace the water to keep it warm. Refrigerate it for up to a week. Be sure to allow sufficient preparation time for the *crème fraîche*. Yields about 2 cups.

Crème Pâtissière
Pastry Cream

1 cup milk - 150 ml
1/2 vanilla bean
3 egg yolks
1/2 cup sugar - 125 ml
1/3 cup flour - 80 ml

In a saucepan, bring the milk to the boil with the vanilla bean. In a bowl, thoroughly mix the egg yolks, sugar and flour. Add the boiling milk and combine well. Return the mixture to the saucepan and slowly bring it to the boil. Continue to boil for 2 to 3 minutes, stirring constantly. Strain the creamy custard through a fine sieve and keep it warm until needed. If the cream is not to be used immediately, sprinkle a little milk or cream, or a little sugar, over the surface to prevent a skin from forming.

Gratin de Pêches Marjorie

A summer dessert, inexpensively prepared, that has two advantages — it can be served hot or cold.

4 peaches with good flavour
a little Kirsch
a little Curaçao
1 tbsp. cornstarch - 15 ml
1 cup milk - 250 ml
1/4 cup sugar - 60 ml
2 egg yolks
1/2 cup whipped cream - 125 ml
1/4 cup brown sugar - 60 ml

Carefully peel the peaches and cut them into thin slices. Arrange the slices in a suitable round glass dish. Flavour them with the Kirsch and Curaçao.

Dissolve the cornstarch in a little milk. Boil the remaining milk and bind with the cornstarch mixture. Mix the egg yolks and sugar together and stir in the boiling milk. Bring this to the boil, strain it and pour into a bowl. Dust the top with sugar to prevent a skin from forming and allow it to cool.

When the mixture is cold, carefully fold in the whipped cream and flavour it with additional Kirsch and Curaçao.

Cover the peaches with the cream, sprinkle with brown sugar and burn a glaze with a hot pastry iron, or place under a hot broiler. (It is very important that the iron or broiler is very hot so that a proper glaze of sugar forms.) Serves 4.

Crêpes aux Noisettes Pancakes with Chocolate and Nut Stuffing

This dish was created for a regional culinary competition.

1/2 cup milk - 125 ml
1/2 cup flour - 125 ml
1 egg yolk
1 whole egg
1 tbsp. sugar - 15 ml
2 tsp. melted butter - 10 ml
2 tsp. butter, for frying the pancakes - 10 ml

Thoroughly mix the milk and flour in a bowl. Add the egg yolk, egg and sugar and mix in well. Add the melted butter and pass the mixture through a sieve. Make very thin pancakes.

Filling
1/2 cup macaroons, crushed - 125 ml
1/2 cup hazelnuts, finely chopped - 125 ml
1/2 cup walnuts, finely chopped - 125 ml
2 cups *crème pâtissière* (vanilla cream) - 500ml
2 tbsp. sugar - 30 ml
2 oz. chocolate, melted - 50 g
1 tbsp. cognac - 15 ml
1/2 cup cream, whipped - 125 ml
1/2 tsp. icing sugar - 2 ml

Mix the macaroons and nuts with the *crème pâtissière*, the sugar, chocolate and cognac. Work in the whipped cream carefully. Fill the pancakes with this mixture, cover with buttered paper and warm them in the oven. It's a good idea to pour a little melted butter on the pancakes before warming them in the oven. Sprinkle them with icing sugar just before serving. Serves 4.

Flan
Caramel Custard

1/2 cup plus 4 tsp. sugar - 125 + 20 ml
peel of 1 orange
peel of 1 lemon
2 cups of milk - 500 ml
1 stick cinnamon
2 eggs
1 teaspoon vanilla extract - 5 ml

Caramel

In a small, heavy-bottomed saucepan, place the 1/2 cup of sugar with just enough cold water to cover it. Set over moderate heat. Dip a pastry brush into cold water every minute or so and brush down any sugar crystals that form on the sides of the pan. Allow the sugar to boil undisturbed until it turns a light golden colour. Remove immediately from the heat (be careful, the caramel will be very hot). Divide the caramel among 4 small ramekins or molds holding 6 to 8 fluid ounces each, or pour it into a single, 3-cup mold. Set aside.

Preheat the oven to 350°F(175°C). Bring a kettle of water to a simmer.

Custard

While the caramel is cooking, peel the orange and lemon, leaving the white pith on the fruit. Combine the thin peels with the milk in a saucepan and add the cinnamon stick. Bring to a boil, lower the heat and simmer the mixture for 5 minutes.

Beat the eggs, lightly, then beat in the remaining 4 tsp. of sugar and the vanilla. Slowly beat in the hot milk, then beat for a moment until blended. Strain the custard into the caramel-coated mold or molds. Place them in a roasting pan and pour in enough simmering water to come two-thirds up the sides of the molds.

Bake for 25 to 45 minutes, depending on the size of the molds or until the centre of the custard is just set. Remove the custard from the water bath and cool. Chill. Unmold to serve. Serves 4.

Floating Island
Ile Flottante

A preparation which is absolutely marvelous. Once you have mastered the floating islands, you can accompany them with any type of sauce. This is a refreshing dish to serve all year long.

4 cups milk - 1 L
1 vanilla bean
8 eggs, separated
2 cups sugar - 500 ml
1/4 cup water - 60 ml
1/2 cup sliced almonds (optional) - 125 ml
2 cups raspberries (optional) - .5 L

In a large, wide saucepan, bring the milk and the vanilla bean to a simmer.

Beat the egg whites until soft peaks form. Gradually beat in 1/4 cup of sugar and continue beating until they are stiff. Scoop up several large spoonfuls and poach them on top of the simmering milk, for 3 minutes on each side. Remove them with a slotted spoon and place on a platter. Repeat until all the egg whites have been used. Refrigerate until ready to serve them.

Make a *crème anglaise* (see the recipe in this chapter).

Then, in a small saucepan, combine the 1/4 cup of water and remaining 1/2 cup of sugar. Over moderately high heat, cook until the sugar has completely dissolved. Continue cooking until the syrup turns a light brown (this should take 3 to 4 minutes).

Remove the saucepan from the heat as soon as the desired colour is reached. Immediately pour it over the chilled meringues. (The caramel will have a bitter taste if it darkens too much.)

For the presentation, carefully pour the *crème anglaise* into a serving bowl. Arrange the meringues on top and sprinkle them with almonds. Surround them with raspberries. Serves 6.

Fruit *Douceur*

A recipe which made me a national winner in 1982. Try this just for a challenge.

4 cups vanilla ice cream - 1 L
(to prepare 6 large scoops)
1 orange
1 lemon
5 kiwi fruit
3 large pears
2 cups fruit sugar - 500 ml
1 1/2 cups peeled green pistachio nuts - 375 ml
2 tbsp. gelatin
10 large egg yolks
2 cups whipping cream - 500 ml
2 1/2 cups champagne - 625 ml
fresh mint leaves, for decoration

Syrup
Peel, halve and core the pears. Slice the orange and lemon into sixths. Put 4 cups of water and 1/2 cup of sugar in a saucepan. Bring the mixture slowly to a boil, stirring until the sugar is dissolved. Add the pears, orange and lemon and boil until the pears are barely tender. Remove the pears and cool them. Remove the syrup and discard it.

Sabayon
Heat the champagne in a pot, enough to infuse 1 1/2 cups of chopped and crushed pistachio nuts. Do not allow it to boil. Reserve a few chopped pistachio nuts for garnish in the final preparation.

Soak the gelatin in water and set aside. In a *bain-marie* whisk 10 egg yolks with 1 1/2 cups of sugar until it reaches the ribbon stage. Then remove the mixture from the *bain-marie* and add the infused, warm champagne liquid, including pistachio nuts, to the egg yolk mixture. Add the gelatin to the warm *saybayon*. Mix to melt the gelatin. Strain the mixture into a chilled bowl set in a bed of ice.

Presentation

Place a large scoop of ice cream on each of 6 chilled dessert plates. Set aside a thin slice of each pear half for garnish. Place the pear halves on dessert plates. Peel and cut each kiwi into thin slices, reserving only the uniform slices for garnish. Arrange 4 or 5 slices of kiwi on each plate.

In a chilled bowl, whip the cream until it is firm. Remove 8 tbsp. to another chilled bowl. Fold the remaining cream into the *sabayon*, noting the thick texture. Pour it slowly over the assembled fruit and ice cream until they are covered.

To make a whipped cream *quenelle*, fill a glass with boiling water, dip a dessert spoon in the hot water and scoop out one heaping spoonful of the reserved cream and form it into a dumpling or *quenelle* shape. Make 5 or more *quenelles* and arrange them on the dessert plates with the ice cream and fruit. Garnish each plate with a slice of pear and kiwi, chopped pistachio and fresh mint leaves. Serve immediately. Serves 6.

Hard Berry Cake

The term "hard berry" comes from the late Beatrice Ross Buszek, of the cranberry, blueberry, maple connection cookbooks. She said, "Often strawberries do have a hard shape."

1 cup fresh or frozen strawberries for cake - 250 ml
1 cup fresh or frozen strawberries for sauce - 250 ml
1/2 cup sugar - 125 ml
5 tbsp. gelatin
1 oz. Kirsch - 28 ml
1 cup whipping cream - 250 ml
sponge cake, 4 circles - 3" round by 3/4 " high
ice
fresh mint leaves

Reserving 4 of the best berries for the garnish, purée 1 cup of strawberries. Dissolve the gelatin in water and add to the the purée. Set aside 10 tbsp. of the mixture to use for a final glaze. On a bed of ice, vigorously whip the cream until it is firm. Blend in the sugar and Kirsch.

Place the 4 circles of sponge cake in the bottom of 4 metal rings 3/4 inch high by 3 inches in diameter. Blend the cream mixture with the strawberry purée until it is slightly thickened. Then pour the mixture equally into each ring. Put them in the refrigerator for 4 hours. Once chilled, gently brush the remaining 10 tbsp. of purée onto the cakes as a glaze. Chill again, then carefully remove the metal rings.

Blend the remaining 1 cup of strawberries at slow speed in a blender and pour the sauce around each cake. Garnish with a sprig of fresh mint. Serves 4.

Pastry Cream

An all-purpose pastry cream that can be used to fill pastries such as cream puffs, *feuilletés and Napoleons*.

4 cups milk - 1 L
1 vanilla bean, split lengthwise
12 egg yolks
1 1/3 cups sugar - 330 ml
3/4 cup unsifted flour - 180 ml
1 tsp. unsalted butter - 5 ml

In a large saucepan, bring the milk and vanilla bean to a simmer. Turn off the heat, cover the pan and let it steep for 20 minutes. Remove the vanilla bean.

In a large mixing bowl, using a wire whisk, whip the egg yolks and sugar until pale lemon in colour. Sift in the flour and stir with the whisk. Heat the milk and slowly pour it into the egg yolk mixture, whisking constantly.

Return the contents of the bowl to the saucepan and over medium heat, bring it to a boil. Continue to beat with the whisk until the mixture thickens and boils for 1 minute.

Transfer the pastry cream to a bowl and dot it with butter to avoid a crust from forming. Chill the cream. It will keep for 3 to 4 days when refrigerated. If a lighter cream is desired, fold in whipped cream. Yields a generous 4 cups.

Pâte à Choux
Cream Puff Pastry

Pâte à choux is one of the mother doughs of French pastry making. Choux pastry is always made with what is called a *panade*, a combination of water, butter and flour to which eggs are added.

1 cup water - 250 ml
4 tbsp. unsalted butter - 60 ml
1/4 tsp. salt - 1 ml
1 cup all-purpose flour - 250 ml
4 large eggs

Place the water, butter (cut into pieces) and salt in a heavy saucepan. Bring to a boil. When the butter is completely melted, remove from the heat and add the flour all at once. Mix rapidly with a wooden spoon.

Place the mixture on low heat and "dry" it for 5 to 6 minutes, mixing with the wooden spoon. The dough should be soft and should not stick to your fingers when pinched. This mixture is called the *panade*.

Transfer the *panade* to a clean bowl. You will notice that the bottom of the pan is covered with a thin crust, an indication that the dough has been sufficiently dried.

Let the dough cool for at least 5 minutes. Add the eggs one at a time, beating carefully after each addition so that the mixture is smooth before the next egg is added. The dough should be smooth, shiny and as thick and as heavy as mayonnaise. Yields enough dough for 14 to 16 *choux* or *éclairs*.

Choux and Eclairs

Great companions for afternoon tea. The only difference between a *choux* and an *éclair* is that the former is round and the latter is long. Both can be filled with flavoured whipped cream, *crème patissière*, ice cream, jam and the like.

Pâte à choux
1 egg, beaten
filling (whipped cream, ice cream, etc.)

Prepare the *pâte à choux* following the technique in the preceding recipe. Fill a pastry bag with the dough and coat a large cookie sheet with butter and flour. Squeeze out either puffs about the size of a golf ball or elongated *éclairs*.

Brush the tops with an egg wash (1 whole egg, beaten), pushing down the "tails" that have formed on top. The choux can also be formed by dropping spoonfuls of dough onto the cookie sheet.

Drag the tines of a fork across the top of the unbaked *éclairs* to make a design. Let the *choux* and *éclairs* dry for at least 20 minutes before cooking them. (The egg wash gives them a shiny glaze if it is allowed to dry for a while before baking.)

Bake at 370°F(190°C) in preheated oven for 35 minutes, or until well puffed and golden. Turn off the heat, open the oven door halfway (to let any steam escape) and allow the puffs to cool slowly and dry for an hour. *Pâte à choux* will soften and collapse if they cool too quickly. Cut them into halves to fill or, if desired, keep them whole. Yields 14 to 16 *choux* or *éclairs*.

Puff Pastry

This is an extremely versatile pastry. I recommend preparing a large amount at one time and cutting it into desired quantities and shapes for freezing. It freezes very successfully, but remove it from the freezer and place in the refrigerator the day before you plan to use it.

Détrempe
1 cup pastry flour - 250 ml
1 cup all-purpose flour - 250 ml
1/4 to 1/2 cup unsalted butter, - 60 to 125 ml
(chilled and cut into 6 pieces)
2 tsp. salt - 10 ml
3/4-1 cup ice water - 180-250 ml

Pastry butter for rolling
1 1/4 cups unsalted butter, chilled - 310 ml
1/4 cup all-purpose flour - 60 ml

To make the *détrempe*, combine the pastry flour, all-purpose flour, butter and salt in a food processor or in an electric mixer. Process until the mixture resembles coarse meal.

With the machine running, add just enough ice water to make a stiff but pliable dough. Shape it into a flattened ball and wrap it tightly in plastic wrap. Refrigerate for 30 minutes.

Remove the butter for rolling from the refrigerator. Sprinkle it with flour and knead until soft but still cold. Shape it into a rectangular block, approximately 6 inches by 9 inches.

Remove the *détrempe* from the refrigerator. Cut a deep cross in the dough. Spread out the sections of dough so that the centre is the thickest part. Roll it in opposite directions to form a four-leaved clover, keeping the centre thicker than the edges. Place the block of butter diagonally in the centre of the cloverleaf and bring the edges of the *détrempe* to the centre, enclosing the butter completely. Wrap the dough tightly in plastic wrap and chill it for an hour.

To make the "turns," place the chilled dough on a lightly floured surface. Pound it lightly and evenly with a rolling pin to make the dough pliable. Roll it out into a rectangle approximately 9 inches by 16 inches. With the 9-inch side in front of you, fold it into thirds, starting with the bottom third and folding over the top third. You have now completed the first turn.

Turn the dough so that the narrow end faces you, keeping the seam on your right (a quarter turn). Again, roll out the dough into a rectangle approximately 9 inches by 16 inches and again fold it into thirds. You have now completed two turns. Wrap the dough in plastic wrap and refrigerate it for 30 minutes.

Pound the dough evenly and again roll it out into a 9-inch by 16-inch rectangle. Complete two more turns as above, to make four turns. Wrap the dough in plastic wrap and refrigerate it for 50 to 60 minutes. Repeat the procedure for two more turns to make a total of six turns. Refrigerate until needed.

Use the dough for various recipes as desired. It may be frozen successfully for up to six months if wrapped airtight. Yields 2 1/2 lbs. of pastry.

Thoughts on making the pastry

• Do not overwork the *détrempe* or it will be impossible to roll out. If the *détrempe* is rubbery and not pliable, it is best to toss it out and begin again.

• When making the butter and *détrempe* package, the two parts should be the same temperature and consistency.

• As you roll and turn the pastry, use as little flour as possible, brushing away excess flour with a large pastry brush.

• The chilling times are approximate; the important thing to remember is that the pastry should be chilled all the way through and have sufficient time to rest between turns.

• After the first two turns, it is possible to refrigerate the pastry overnight and then continue with the remaining turns.

Short Pastry

You can use this crumbly, light, delicate pastry as a substitute for puff pastry. It is especially good for meat or fish *en croûte*. It can also serve as the crust for *pâté en croûte*. Traditionally, however, it is the base for flans and tartlets. Short pastry will keep for several days in the refrigerator.

1 1/2 cups all-purpose flour - 375 ml
3/4 cup butter - 180 ml
1 egg
pinch of castor sugar (extra-fine granulated)
1 tsp. fine salt - 5 ml
1 tbsp. milk - 15 ml

Put the flour on a pastry board and make a well in the centre. Cut the slightly softened butter into small pieces and put them into the well together with the egg, sugar and salt. Mix in all the ingredients with the fingertips of your right hand. Use your left hand to push small quantities of flour into the centre of the well as it will tend to spread.

When the ingredients are well mixed, add the cold milk. Knead the pastry two or three times to mix very thoroughly. Wrap it in waxed paper and chill it in the refrigerator for several hours. Depending upon its use, baking time is approximately 20 to 30 minutes. Yields about 1 lb. of pastry.

Chocolate Bread Pudding

8 slices (5 oz.) challah or *brioche* - 142 g
3/4 cup heavy cream - 180 ml
6 ozs. bittersweet chocolate, cut into pieces - 151 g
1/2 cup + 3 tbsp. butter, - 125 + 45 ml
(at room temperature)
5 eggs, separated
3/4 cup almonds, finely ground - 180 ml
1 cup sugar - 250 ml

Preheat the oven to 350°F(175°C). Butter 12 half-cup molds. Combine the challah or *brioche* with the heavy cream and let it stand for 30 minutes. Melt the chocolate over a *bain-marie*. Let it cool and set it aside.

Cream the butter in a food processor or a large mixing bowl. Add the egg yolks, almonds, 3/4 cup of sugar, the soaked bread (challah) and the melted chocolate. Process until it is well combined. Whip the egg whites until soft peaks form. Gradually beat in the remaining 1/4 cup of sugar and continue to beat until they are stiff and shiny. Fold them into the chocolate mixture. Pour this into the prepared molds and set them in a *bain-marie*. Cover loosely with buttered foil, buttered side down. Bake the molds for 45 to 50 minutes, or until they are set.

Whip the heavy cream with the sugar, only to the chantilly stage (the consistency of a mousse).

Serve with the chantilly cream and additional *crème anglaise* (see the recipe in this chapter) which can be placed around the unmolded cakes on the serving plates. Serves 12.

Pear *Frangipane*

An exciting recipe which is always good to serve during the winter months. You can flavour it slightly with gin, vodka or cognac.

4 Bartlett pears
2 cups red wine - 500 ml
1 cup sugar - 250 ml
1/2 stick cinnamon
3 anise stars
1 lemon
1/2 orange
mint leaves

Peel the pears. Combine the wine, sugar, cinnamon, mint, lemon, orange and anise stars with 2 cups of water. (You can find anise stars in health food shops.) Place the pears in the water and cook them slowly for 10 minutes. Remove the pears and put them on ice.

Frangipane preparation
1/2 cup butter - 125 ml
1 cup sugar - 250 ml
3 cups almonds - 750 ml
2 eggs
2 oz. gin (1/4 cup)

Cut the pears into a fan shape and place each in the centre of a large plate. Coat the pears with the *frangipane* sauce and set them aside for 5 minutes. Place under a broiler and glaze until they are golden brown. Dress with icing sugar and serve. Serves 4.

Vanilla Ice Cream

3 cups half and half cream (blend) - 750 ml
1 cup sugar - 250 ml
4 egg yolks, well beaten
1 cup whipping cream - 250 ml
1 tbsp. vanilla extract

In a heavy medium-sized saucepan, combine the cream, sugar and well-beaten egg yolks. Cook over low heat, stirring until the mixture thickens slightly and coats a metal spoon. Cool to room temperature. Stir in the whipping cream and vanilla. Pour into the canister of an ice cream maker and freeze it according to the manufacturer's directions. Yields 2 quarts or 8 cups.

Old-fashioned Vanilla Ice Cream

1 1/3 cups sugar - 330 ml
1 tbsp. cornstarch - 15 ml
1/4 tsp. salt - 1 ml
3 cups whole milk - 750 ml
2 egg yolks
1/3 cup evaporated milk - ? ml
1 cup whipping cream - 250 ml
1 tbsp. vanilla extract - 15 ml

In a medium-sized saucepan, combine the sugar, cornstarch and salt. Stir in the whole milk. Place on medium heat, stirring constantly until the mixture begins to simmer. Simmer for 1 minute over low heat and set aside. In a small bowl, lightly beat the egg yolks. Stir 1 cup of the milk mixture into the egg yolks, stir the egg yolk mixture into the remaining milk mixture. Cook and stir over low heat for 2 minutes, or until it is slightly thickened. Stir in the evaporated milk, whipping cream and vanilla. Cool the mixture to room temperature. Pour into the canister of an ice cream maker and freeze it according to the manufacturer's directions. Yields 2 quarts or 8 cups.

Royal Crown Vanilla Ice Cream

5 egg yolks
2/3 cup sugar - 165 ml
1 cup half and half cream (blend) - 250 ml
2 tbsp. butter - 30 ml
1 cup whipping cream - 250 ml
2 tsp. vanilla extract - 10 ml

In a medium-sized bowl, beat the egg yolks and sugar until well blended. Pour into the top part of a double boiler. Stir in the cream. Cook the mixture and stir it over gently boiling water until it thickens. Set aside. Stir in the butter. Stirring occasionally, cool on a rack to room temperature. Stir in the whipping cream and vanilla. Pour into the canister of an ice cream maker and freeze it according to the manufacturer's directions. Yields 1 quart or 4 cups.

Tarte Tatin

1 1/2 cups unsalted butter - 375 ml
1/2 cup sugar - 125 ml
2 lbs. apples - 908 g
2 scant cups flour - 500 ml
1 egg
pinch salt

Using 7 tbsp. of the butter, generously grease the bottom of a 9-inch cast-iron frying pan. Then sprinkle half of the sugar into it.

Peel the apples, dry them with a cloth, core and cut them into quarters or thick slices. Arrange the apple pieces together tightly to cover the bottom of the pan. Sprinkle the remaining sugar on top of them. Add 1 1/2 tbsp. of melted butter.

Place the pan on the stove over high heat for about 20 minutes keeping a close eye to make sure it does not burn, just long enough to allow the sugar to caramelize but also to remain light brown in colour.

Mound the flour on a pastry board. Form a well in the centre of the flour and in it place the egg, the salt and the remaining butter, softened. Mix all the ingredients together. Add some water, if necessary, to produce a soft dough that can be rolled as thinly as possible into a circle.

Cover the pan with this dough, pushing the edges inside the pan. Bake in a pre-heated 325°F(165°C) oven for 30 minutes. Invert the *tarte tatin* onto a serving platter. Let it cool before serving. You can substitute the apple with pears or mangoes, or even pineapple. Serves 6.

Culinary Terms

Armagnac: A type of brandy similar to a cognac

Bain-marie: A double-boiler

Beurre blanc: A white foamy butter sauce

Blanched: Ingredients, usually vegetables, gradually brought to the boil in water, often to remove the skins

Bouquet garni: Aromatic herbs or plants tied together in a small bunch, mainly made up of leeks, celery and thyme

Brioche: A cake made out of yeast dough, used for a great many dishes, especially pastries

Brunoise: Vegetables cut into a small dice

Butter paper: Waxed paper

Butter, sweet: Unsalted butter

Capers: The pickled floral bud of the caper bush, used as a seasoning and condiment

Celeraic: A variety of celery with a large edible root

Chantilly stage: Cream that is beaten to the consistency of a mousse

Chiffonade: A mixture of lettuces or sorrel, cut into thin strips and cooked in butter for soup garnish

Chinois: A conical strainer with a fine mesh

Concassé: Roughly chopped

Cornichon: A small pickle, gherkin

Crème fraîche: A naturally fermented thick cream

Croustade: A hollow pastry shell or bread ready to be filled with various preparations

Dariole mold: A small cylindrical mold named after a small pastry

Déglaçer: To deglaze, or dilute concentrated cooking juices in a pan in which meat, poultry, game or fish has been roasted, braised or fried. Wine, soup, stock or cream may be used.

Demi-glace: A brown sauce, usually flavoured with Madeira or sherry

Détrempe: A technical confectionery term meaning a mixture of flour and water that is used in the preparation of pastries, mainly for puff pastry

Double cream: Heavy cream containing a high fat content

Duxelles: A coarse paste or hash made with finely chopped mushrooms and sautéed with shallots

Feuilleté: A puff pastry dough that is difficult to make. The correct folding of the dough is the key to obtaining the proper rising.

Fish fumet: The stock made from the bones and trimmings of fish, very reduced and often used with white wine in the cooking of certain fish

Fleuron: A small flaky pastry design used to decorate certain dishes; lozenges, crescents or other shapes made with puff pastry

Glaze: The liquid with a syrupy consistency and glossy appearance often used to coat and garnish foods in cold preparations only

Infusion: The steeping in boiling liquid to obtain various flavours, such as a vanilla bean in milk or mushrooms in wine

Julienne: Vegetables cut into match-shaped rods

Marron: A species of chestnut whose fruit contains only a single nut

Madrilène: A consommé flavoured with tomato, usually served chilled or cold

Mirepoix: A mixture of carrots, onions, fresh bacon and ham cut into a dice and used as base for sauces

Mousselines: Molds made from pastes of poultry, game, fish or shellfish and enriched with cream. They are served either hot or cold and when chilled are known as aspics.

Nap: To coat the back of a spoon with a hot, thick liquid

Papillote: Foods cooked *en papillote* are steamed in the oven in a piece of heart-shaped parchment paper.

Paysanne: Uniformly cut meat and poultry prepared by braising and accompanied by a garnish of carrots, turnips, onions, celery and potatoes cooked in butter.

Petite marmite: A clear savoury broth or type of hot-pot with various mirepoix

Pernod: A licorice-flavoured liqueur produced in France

Quenelle: A dumpling shape prepared by repeatedly changing the mixture one spoon to another as many times as needed in order to obtain the desired shape

Ramekins: The type of mold used for various cuisine preparations

Ribbon: A sugar and egg yolk mixture, well beaten, which forms ribbon-like folds when dropped from the spoon

Salamander: A broiler

Sauteuse: A shallow casserole or high-sided frying pan

Sorrel: A perennial herb whose young leaves are used as salad greens or as a vegetable

Sweat: To toss quickly in a hot fat any meats or vegetables in order to colour them before moistening.

Terrine: An earthenware dish in which meat, game and fish are cooked; also the food itself

Truffle: A subterranean fungus, of which a number of varieties exist; a delicacy used in French cuisine

White Stock: Or, *fond blanc*, a colourless chicken or veal stock

INDEX